Japan in the Global Community

JAPAN
IN THE GLOBAL
COMMUNITY

Its Role and Contribution on the Eve of the 21st Century

Edited by
Yasusuke Murakami
Yutaka Kosai

Round Table Discussions on Japan in the Global Community
Distributed by UNIVERSITY OF TOKYO PRESS

© Round Table Discussions on Japan in the Global Community, 1986

Distributed by University of Tokyo Press
ISBN 4–13–057014–5 UTP 57148
ISBN 0–86008–405–1

Printed in Japan

Contents

**Part II Japan's Role in and Contribution to the
Global Community**

Foreword

Industrial society, which has grown and evolved from the time of the Industrial Revolution in the 18th century, is today at a historical turning point; the prolonged stability that characterized the world economic and political systems in the early decades following World War II is also beginning to change. Meanwhile, developments in industry and trade are creating rapidly tightening bonds of global interdependence, contributing, in turn, both to improved understanding among nations and, at the same time, to the proliferation of various kinds of bilateral and multilateral friction. The international situation, therefore, is becoming increasingly fluid and multipolar, not only in the economic realm but politically, culturally, and in every other respect.

Cooperation among all the nations of the world is needed today in order to achieve peace and prosperity in the global community in the years leading up to the turn of the 21st century.

In recognition of this fundamental need and in view of the changes occurring in Japan's status and role in international society in recent years, the Ministry of International Trade and Industry (MITI) organized a series of Round Table Discussions on "Japan in the Global Community." First convened in September 1985, the group met repeatedly to consider Japan's role in the global community and the ways it can contribute to a better world in the period from now through the early part of the 21st century.

The discussants were 26 experts from various fields, 16 from Japan and 10 from other countries, and the result was a lively interdisciplinary exchange presented from diverse historical as well as global viewpoints. Such wide-ranging discussions concerning Japan's role and policies for the future were the first of their kind attempted in Japan. Nevertheless, thanks to the broad knowledge and expertise of the participants, the discussions were extremely fruitful, culminating in certain basic points of agreement which were set forth in the group's final report. As chairman of the discussions, I am pleased and proud that our collective efforts thus led to the firm consensus described in the pages that follow.

It is clear that, in this period of historical transition, we can no longer afford short-term, wait-and-see responses and adjustments; it has become extremely important for us to formulate entirely new ideas based on a long-term and broad perspective. The Japanese people and their government need consistent principles with which to approach the new phase in the world economy and to gain a better understanding of their position by other members of the international community. I believe that this volume is a historic document that will serve to provoke a fundamental change in policies and principles. It is the firm and unanimous conviction of all the members of the round-table discussions that the Japanese economy and society must change in accordance with the directions indicated in this report. It is my impression, furthermore, judging from the results of recent opinion polls and other data, that many Japanese, particularly those of the younger generation, are beginning to feel the urgent need for Japan to turn in the direction of greater internationalism.

Today, Japan must clearly recognize its status in the world, consider its proper role in and contribution to the international community in a long-term perspective that reaches well into the 21st century, and make active efforts as a responsible member of the group of advanced nations. This report is intended to clarify the conceptual framework and fundamental premises upon which such efforts can be based. We hope that the report will prompt renewed and lively debate at diverse levels—among individuals, within corporations, and within the government—in order to assure that concrete and steady steps are made toward realization of the goals described herein.

September 1986   Yasusuke Murakami
Chairman, Round Table Discussions on
Japan in the Global Community

ROUND TABLE DISCUSSIONS ON JAPAN IN THE GLOBAL COMMUNITY

List of Members

Chairman
Murakami, Yasusuke (Japan)

Professor of Economics, University of Tokyo

Deputy Chairman
Kosai, Yutaka (Japan)

Professor of Economics, Tokyo Institute of Technology

(Alphabetical Order)

Aki, Yoko (Japan)	Lyricist
Berger, François (France)	Chairman, Pechiney Japon
Clark, Gregory (Australia)	Professor of Economics and International Business, Sophia University
Garten, Jeffrey E. (USA)	Managing Director, Shearson Lehman Brothers Asia Inc.
Han, Sung-joo (Korea)	Professor of Political Science, Korea University
Hupperts, Isabelle (Belgium)	Representative, Baring Brothers & Co., Ltd.
Inoki, Takenori (Japan)	Associate Professor of Labor Economics, Osaka University
Itami, Hiroyuki (Japan)	Professor of Management, Hitotsubashi University
Ito, Motoshige (Japan)	Associate Professor of International Finance and International Trade, University of Tokyo
Iwao, Sumiko (Japan)	Professor of Social Psychology, Keio University
Kobayashi, Yotaro (Japan)	President, Fuji Xerox Co., Ltd.
Kojima, Akira (Japan)	Editorial Writer, Nihon Keizai Shimbun Inc.
Lee, Kuo Ching (China)	President, Pacific Economic Review
Loughran, John F. (USA)	Vice Chairman, Morgan Guaranty Ltd.

xiv

Murakami, Yoichiro (Japan)	Professor of History and Philosophy of Science, University of Tokyo
Nasution, Anwar (Indonesia)	Research Associate, Institute of Economic & Social Studies, Faculty of Economics, Indonesia University
Okabe, Yoichi (Japan)	Associate Professor of Electronics, University of Tokyo
Osborn, Jack L. (USA)	Vice President Asia/Pacific, TRW Overseas Inc.
Pearce, Robert V. (UK)	Director, Cornes & Co., Ltd.
Sakaiya, Taichi (Japan)	President, The Asian Club Foundation; Writer
Yamakage, Susumu (Japan)	Associate Professor of International Relations, University of Tokyo
Yamamoto, Kozo (Japan)	Principal Architect/Director, Kenzo Tange Associates
Yamamoto, Yoshinobu (Japan)	Professor of International Relations, Saitama University
Yamazaki, Masakazu (Japan)	Professor of Aesthetics and Drama, Osaka University; Writer

Preface

Today's international scene is becoming more fluid and multipolar. More than ever, the cooperation of all countries is needed if the world, as a global community, is to enjoy peace and prosperity as it enters the 21st century. It is imperative that Japan, as a member of this community, seriously consider its role and the kind of positive contribution it can make.

The Round Table Discussion on Japan in the Global Community convened in September 1985 by Vice Minister Keiichi Konaga of the Ministry of International Trade and Industry, and was charged with examining the role and contribution of Japan in the global community from the present through the first half of the 21st century. Professor Yasusuke Murakami of the University of Tokyo was chairman of the Discussion, and Professor Yutaka Kosai served as deputy chairman. The basic approach was to consider a wide range of issues from a long-term, inter-disciplinary perspective. To facilitate this, 26 experts in various fields, from both Japan and other countries, were invited to participate. (The names of the participants are listed below.)

Procedures

Eight conferences were held, the first in September 1985 and the last in April 1986. Each of the monthly meetings took up a prearranged theme, with two or three members selected in advance to present papers, copies of which were distributed to the other members beforehand. (Topics discussed at each meeting are listed below.)

Each Round Table Discussion began with the paper presentations, followed by reactions from two or three commentators selected beforehand; general discussion ensued, with all members participating in a lively exchange of views.

At the end of February 1986, the specific research themes were grouped into three broad areas: international politics, economics and business, and culture. The members were organized into small working groups, discussing each of these areas intensively. The overall theme of these discussions thus was not narrowly economic, but encompassed international politics as well as social and cultural factors.

Final Report

Part I places "Japan in the 21st century" in a historical perspective and tries to assess its economic, political, and cultural roles in the broad context of global trends. Building on this, Part II first deals with the basic conceptual framework that should inform Japan as it faces the next century. It then suggests concrete ways through which these basic concepts can be realized. The seven issue areas thus brought out represent those that attracted concern and prolonged discussion among the members instead of being a systematic and exhaustive treatment of the topic. In discussing the posture that Japan should adopt in facing the world in the 21st century, members of the discussion group, especially the Japanese members, came up with various suggestions regarding the life, value system, and internationalization of the Japanese people.

Part III sums up the preceding discussion by focusing on the Japanese people, the actual participants in "Japan in the Global Community: On the Eve of the 21st Century." While expressing the hope that the Japanese, although not conscious of the word "internationalization," can come to an understanding of the world without changing their basic character.

Points that could not be considered fully in the course of the Discussions or on which some members could not agree with the consensus arrived at by other members, or on which strong minority opinions were expressed, have been noted in the text, and the dissenting opinions are summarized in notes at the end of the section.

The basic purpose of this reports is to propose an ideal future direction for Japan and to point out a general path towards that ideal. Although some of the basic tone is more theoretical than applicational, gaps between theory and reality were also given due consideration. It is hoped that this report will serve to stimulate similar discussions around the world, which in turn will open the road toward a true global community in which Japan will prosper together with the other countries of the world.

Japan in the Global Community

PART I

Why Consider Japan in the Global Community?

In considering the subject "Japan in the Global Community on the Eve of the 21st Century," we must first ask what the world —and what Japan—will be like in the next century. In Part I, we outline the process of industrialization in the context of world history and the development of the global system, tracing their interrelationship, in order to gain a perspective on international society in the coming 20 to 30 years. We then seek a global perspective on how the international system and industrial society will change on the eve of the 21st century, and explore the relevance of "Japan in the Global Community" to our times. We also try to provide a historical perspective on modern Japan, considering how its culture has interacted with and has been affected by the recent transformation of industrial society and the world system.

A. The Transformation of Industrial Society and the International System

1. Technological Innovation and the Transformation of Industrial Society

The concept of the world as encompassing the entire planet Earth did not become established in the true sense until the age of the great voyages in the 16th century. We may also say that the prototype of the contemporary world system, shaped by political, military, and economic factors, emerged only with the Industrial Revolution that began in the late 18th century.

Columbus, Magellan, and the other great voyagers not only carved out a whole new geographical image of the world; they opened up the frontiers of the world economy. The first Industrial Revolution in Great Britain spawned new types of industries that sought raw materials and markets throughout the world, across national boundaries. That, in turn, created an economic dynamism that opened up further frontiers in the world economy. With this, the weight carried by the economy in the international system increased rapidly.

The growth of international economic activities meant that technological innovation, a key factor in economic development, was closely linked to the transformation of the international system. In other words, it meant that those countries that grasped the initiative at each stage of technological innovation and successfully managed to industrialize first were the ones that enjoyed the greatest power in international society and that took the lead in world affairs.

Technological Innovation Since the Industrial Revolution

The introduction of factory production methods using machinery in the textile (spinning) industry heralded the arrival of the Industrial Revolution. Subsequently the steam engine, using coal as fuel, was introduced as a source of energy for production and power for transportation. These developments made possible continuous production on an immense scale that was unthinkable in the days of reliance on manual labor alone. At the same time, the so-called free laborer, who was not chained to the means of production such as land or machinery, came into being, and new industrial activity which sought both raw materials and markets overseas began to develop. Typical of the technological structure of the 19th century were the textile, railroad, shipbuilding, and steelmaking industries, which grew rapidly in that century and formed the core of industrial society until the early part of the 20th century.

At the beginning of the 20th century, steam-generated energy was replaced by electric power, which is relatively easy both to control and to transmit. This was also the period when oil and oil products, the fuel that made possible the rapid development of the internal combustion engine, first came into widespread use. Revolutionary changes in energy resources ushered in an age of new industries centered around the manufacture of electric appliances and automobiles. In these industries, in particular, the main method employed was mass production, which utilized to the fullest the easy controllability of electrical energy; and they reached their peak of development in the decades following World War II. Their products developed, basically, to fill the demand of a huge mass consumer market, and in the process of their diffusion rapid industrial growth of unprecedented proportions took place.

Prospects for Further Technological Innovation

During the 19th and the first three quarters of the 20th century, rising labor-to-capital equipment ratios and rising rates of energy consumption per product unit were consistent trends in industrialization. In other words, the trend was toward large-scale, mass production. In the 1970s, however, profound changes began occurring in this pattern of industrialization.

Today, a new wave of technological innovation is under way as a result of the application of technologies and new materials and of advances in space research, nuclear energy, and many other fields. The common background to this new wave of technological innovation is the revolution in information technology centering on the rapid development of computers and microelectronics. The revolution in information technology has allowed the transmission and control of information, once dependent on human skills, to be conducted in mass volume, in great detail, and at high speed. Information has also become the motive force behind many kinds of technological innovation and diversification of products. Moreover, the information technology revolution is continuing at a rapid pace, and it even appears that by the 21st century technological innovation may come up with substitutes for human powers of intelligence. The current technological innovation centering on developments in information technology represents a great wave that will shift the very vector of technological progress as it has continued since the 19th century.

As the above suggests, technological innovation is primarily a phenomenon on the supply side of industrial society. Now let us look at the changes taking place on the demand side. Consumer demand is, by nature, two-faceted: the consumer is driven by both the desire to have the same thing his neighbor has and the urge to possess that which his neighbor does not have. Mass production and standardization of products are responses to the former impulse, while diversification and the distinctive touch are sustained by the latter urge. Of course, neither of these two facets of consumer demand is such that one will push aside or eliminate the other. Diversification and splintering of interests and groups, moreover, will lead to greater diversity in demand and more rapid change in styles. The emergence of demand for more diversified, distinctive merchandise, however, does not necessarily mean that demand for standardized, mass-produced goods will diminish.

Until recently the main technological innovations on the production side have been related to mass production and standardization, and response to demand for diversification and distinctiveness has been insufficient. This kind of constraint is now being removed by new technologies and other innovation; it has become possible to build a more flexible supply structure, with manufacture of small quantities of diverse types of products.

Overview of the New Industrial Society

Changes in technological conditions and in demand are also altering the relationship between labor and the means of production. We are already observing a drastic increase in the proportion of workers involved in planning and development as compared to those directly engaged in production. From now on, should the relative weight of demand for more diversified, distinctive products rise, we can expect that the weight of sectors in which the knowledge, experience, and information held by workers themselves are the essential means of production will gradually increase. (It is conceivable that, with further innovation in information technology, the function of workers as sources of information will also to a certain extent be taken over by machines.) As this happens, the separation between the means of production and labor which has grown more marked since the Industrial Revolution will be reversed: the two will be integrated once again and the management structure of enterprises will probably change accordingly. In addition, the structure of comparative advantage among nations and the international division of labor are also likely to change.

If the current wave of technological innovation centering on information is indeed backed by a long-latent demand for diversified and distinctive products, the trend will probably be quite steady and its impact extremely widespread: it will affect not only the economic aspect of the international system but also the political and social spheres. It is on the basis of this assumption that the present era is often called the period of transition to post-industrial society, the new industrial revolution, or the age of the information revolution.

Japan in Transition to a New Industrial Society

Japan achieved rapid economic growth after World War II, just at the time when mass-production technology was reaching maturation in the automobile, electrical appliance, and other consumer durables industries; and demand for these products rose rapidly in response. As we shall see below, it was also the period when free trade rapidly expanded and became firmly established. This made it possible for Japan to acquire technology and raw materials comparatively freely, and also allowed the markets for Japanese products to grow rapidly along with the expansion of free trade and the growth of the world economy. In this sense, the world economy following World War II offered Japan an extremely favorable environment. Under these supportive circumstances, Japan was ultimately successful in catching up in development with the Western industrialized countries, eventually taking its place among the leading nations of the world in both technology and economic strength.

Today, when the world is on the verge of experiencing a new industrial revolution and the advent of a new kind of industrial society, Japan must strike out for the frontiers of the new industrial society on its own strength and initiative. Moreover, it is probably safe to say that the kind of new industrial society that Japan builds will have considerable impact on the whole world.

2. Change in Global Management: From Hegemony to Collective Global Management Led by the United States

In the past, major changes in the technological structure invariably wrought changes in the international system as a whole: the country which held the overwhelming advantage in a specific industry or a specific technology that was the key in the technological paradigm for the world's economic development in a given era became the leader of international society and took the initiative in the formation of the international order of that era.

Assuming leadership in international society has always meant bearing a major portion of the various costs involved in maintaining the international order—bearing the burden of supplying international public goods, we might say. From the time of the Industrial Revolution, between the 19th century and the early part of the 20th century, it was Great Britain that shouldered this role, and following World War II, it was the United States. These two countries represented a hegemonic presence in the world, not only economically but politically, culturally, and militarily.

Now, let us examine the specific nature of international public goods and what their supply means in the maintenance of the international order. We shall also take a look at the status of these two countries in the industrial society of the world at the time of their ascendency and at the role they played in global management. On this basis, we may then consider the future system of global management.

The Significance of International Public Goods

International public goods correspond on a world scale to the public goods that exist within each country. The latter include the guarantee of rules for business transactions, the credibility of the currency, and the maintenance of public order; social welfare, public education, and other services are also provided, primarily by the government, and usually their cost is covered by tax revenues.

Various policies covering domestic markets and money supply translate in the international context into the system of world trade and the international monetary system. Domestic public order corresponds on the world scale to international security or stability in international relations. National social welfare has its counterpart internationally in economic assistance, refugee relief, and other such activities. While freedom of economic transactions is in principle guaranteed within each country, free trade is not necessarily a given condition in the international arena, and in this sense maintaining a system of free trade is itself a kind of international public good.

The supply of international public goods in the international system is not guaranteed by any governing body, and is therefore not so well institutionalized as domestic supply of public goods. The supply of international public goods is ordinarily undertaken by international agencies and organizations or by specific countries capable of assuming the burden. It naturally follows, then, that the rules regarding supply of international public goods are by no means explicit and that they lack any binding power.

The Role of Great Britain

The Industrial Revolution in Great Britain began with the textile industry and spread in a chain reaction to the machine industry, steelmaking, and coal mining. In addition, sea and rail transport grew rapidly in response to the increased demand for movement of vast quantities of raw cotton and other raw materials as well as foodstuffs. The development of the railroad industry, in particular, stimulated demand for the steel and other industries.

The basic pattern of economic advance for industrializing nations in the post-Industrial Revolution era was the acquisition of colonial territories to serve both as suppliers of raw materials and as consumer markets for industrial products. At the beginning of the 20th century, in fact, 87 percent of Asia, Africa, and Oceania was under the colonial control of European countries or the United States.

Great Britain, making the most of its head start in the Industrial Revolution, held the lead in the world system by virtue of its supreme economic strength and powerful naval forces. In this period Great Britain exercised control over many parts of the world where the main raw materials were produced; at its height, the volume of Britain's trade accounted for one-third of all world trade. It sustained a current account surplus for more than one hundred years. Great Britain also led the world in technology and played a major role in the dissemination of new industrial technology as well as the gold standard system throughout international society. Britain's global economic and military activities spread free trade, parliamentary democracy, and English as the language of international society.

The Role of the United States

In 1913, the United States established a firm lead in the automobile industry with the development of the mass production system, and was far ahead of any other country in economic strength by the end of World War I. After struggling through the years of turmoil following the Great Depression of 1929 and World War II, the United States established itself as the political leader of the West. It also played the leading role in the creation of the General Agreement on Tariffs and Trade (GATT) and the International Monetary Fund (IMF), which provided the framework for the economic system of the free world in the postwar period. Through the GATT and IMF systems the United States became the main driving force propelling free trade, and by its guarantee of the convertibility of the dollar, it became the sole supplier of international currency. It recycled the immense current accounts surplus thus created in the form of capital export. (Like the U.K. in the 19th century, the U.S. had a continuous current accounts surplus from just after World War I to the 1970s.) In addition, the United States carried one-third of the burden of the cost of the United Nations as of 1960, as well as the greater part of the burden of official development assistance, and played the overriding role in assuring the efficient functioning of various international organizations and the maintenance of the postwar international order. These various forms of contribution to the global welfare were consistent with the national interest of the United States.

American leadership in the economic realm was sustained, as suggested earlier, by rapid advances in the utilization of electrical and petroleum energy and the spread of consumer goods pivoting on these two types of energy. The consumer durables, chiefly automobiles and electrical appliances, were goods that enjoyed a massive consumer market and that were well suited to the large-scale mass production method. They also served as a catalyst for the growth of a broad spectrum of industries, including steel and chemicals. In these industries, the industrial infrastructure of the United States, which boasted a wide technological advantage over all other countries, was extremely strong.

Then, with the adoption of Nixon's "New Economic Policy" in 1971, the Bretton Woods system of currency exchange collapsed, and the dollar ceased to function as the key currency sustaining the fixed exchange rate system. Moreover, many industries in the United States and Europe began to face severe international competition, and today the new threat of protectionism is rearing its ugly head.

The United States remains the most advanced country in the world in many respects. However, with the development and spread of information, communications, and education, the international diffusion of technology became very easy. It became difficult for the U.S. to maintain its technological superiority, and its capacity to supply international public goods was correspondingly diminished.

With technology transfer from the United States, late starters like Japan were not burdened with immense initial costs and were thereby able to raise the standards of their technology with relative ease. This meant that these latecomers were able to catch up technologically with the pioneering nations in a comparatively short period of time.

Another factor in the diminished position of the U.S. on the world stage is the monumental cost of its military burden. Following World War II, a bipolar political and military structure emerged, with the Eastern bloc of nations under the overwhelming leadership of the Soviet Union and the Western bloc centered around the United States. Trying to gain an advantage in this bipolar structure or to stabilize it, the United States could not avoid immense military expenditures, and these expenditures not only served the interests of its Western allies but also helped to lighten their burden of defense outlay.

The Contemporary World System and Directions of Change

The international system that has prevailed since the end of World War II consists of the bipolar East-West structure in the political and military realms, on the one hand, and the economic system based on free trade among the nations of the West, on the other. What this has meant (at least for the Western-bloc countries other than the United States) is that the mechanism of stability in the military realm and that in the economic realm have to a certain extent been independent.

Competition or friction in the economic sphere did not immediately affect relations in the military sphere. For one thing, since the end of World War II, as the leader of the West, the United States has sought in its economic policy to prevent the politicization of economic issues and to solve economic problems within the framework of the free trade system. This policy has proved very successful so far, allowing the world economy to develop despite crises that occurred time and time again. This is clear, for example, from the fact that the most rapid growth of the free market economy coincided with the period from the Cold War in the 1950s through the Vietnam War, and that the confusion in the world economy brought on by the collapse of the Bretton Woods system in 1971 and the oil crisis of 1973 was overcome basically within the framework of economic mechanisms.

It should be recognized that economic or technological changes in the U.S. and the Soviet Union will affect the future military power of these two countries. However, judging from the decided preponderance of the United States and the Soviet Union in political and military affairs at the present time, we may conclude that the bipolar framework of competition between the superpowers will not appreciably change in the remaining years of the 20th century, even though détente will continue to be the hope of the world.

With the growth of the international economy, the burden of public goods necessary to maintain the international economic order has grown ever greater. The increasing military costs notwithstanding, the burden shouldered by the U.S. in providing international public goods has grown excessive. Given this fact, it is natural that other industrialized countries should shoulder some of the burden of supplying international public goods.

The Shift to a Collective Management System

Instability in the world economic order is growing. The economic interests of industrialized countries are at odds in many industries, and in the areas in which the advanced nations are losing their comparative advantage, international frictions involving developing countries are growing acute. Under these circumstances, it is all the more important to maintain and develop the free economic system that made postwar prosperity possible and to further augment the various kinds of economic apparatus that have sustained it, thereby preventing the world economy from heading in the direction of a contracted equilibrium.

In managing the world economic system from now on, each of the advanced nations of the West will have to actively assume a share of the burden of supplying international public goods and to move toward a collective management system, making decisions on various issues through consultation and adjustment of interests and opinions. Naturally, with its overall strength, the United States will continue to play the leading role in the collective management system.

In an age when corporations are active across national boundaries, goods and capital are freely exchanged internationally, and even the allocation of production facilities is determined internationally, it is exceedingly difficult for the nations involved to adjust conflicting interests at home for the sake of keeping up with growing internationalization. This is because a nation-state continues to be an entity based on such less transferable elements as people and land. However, if each country accepts its share of the responsibility and assumes a greater burden than in the past, and the maintenance of the international order thereby becomes easier, the ultimate benefit to the nations of the West will probably be far greater than the cost. The summit meetings of the leaders of the industrialized democracies and the efforts of the Group of Five are steps in that direction.

Given the context of these changes in the world system, it is clear that Japan, which has taken for granted stability in the international economic and political systems and acted on the assumption that it is a "minor power," is facing the need to revise this basic assumption.

Japan's goals in the postwar period have been chiefly of an economic nature, and the nation has sought its identity and strength within international society primarily in economic terms. By the mid-1950s, the Japanese economy had recovered to its prewar high, and, following the rapid growth period of the 1960s, it was strong enough to ride out the challenges of the two oil crises in the 1970s. Today, Japan's economy compares favorably with that of any other advanced nation, and it accounts for 10 percent of the world's GNP; at least economically speaking, Japan's impact on the world, on both the supply and demand sides, is considerable. In these respects alone, Japan can no longer afford to follow the logic of a "minor power."

3. Increasing Interdependence: Growing Awareness of the Global Community

The rapid development of industrial society and the postwar system of free trade led by the United States served to strikingly increase the volume of exchange among nations. As a result of revolutionary developments in communications and transportation technology, the movement of capital, and trade liberalization, the nations of the world have grown much closer in time and space, and enterprises are operating on an international scale. Thus the interdependence among them, in both qualitative and quantitative terms, has deepened. This is true not only in the economy, but also in the realms of culture and society. It affects relations among the industrialized nations as well as those between countries of the North and South and of the East and West. To give a few concrete examples demonstrating the diverse ways that international interdependence has increased, we may note that in the past 15 years alone, the volume of world trade has increased almost sevenfold, the balance of direct investment overseas by the industrialized countries has risen almost fourfold, and the amount of technology trade among the major nations has increased threefold. International telephone calls and electronic data transmissions have jumped tens, even hundreds of times over the level in the early 1970s.

The expansion of various forms of international interchange and the resulting changes in every dimension of international society is affecting all nations. While, on the one hand, these developments are deepening international understanding and helping to further promote exchange, on the other they are provoking a variety of both domestic and external frictions, conflicts, and disputes. This situation only shows more clearly how great the need will be, in implementing the hoped-for collective management system, for even more multidimensional considerations. Now let us examine the impact of deepening interdependence and the directions of change in international society.

Deepening Interdependence and the Growth of Friction

Frictions, conflicts, and disputes among countries are extremely diverse. They include disputes among private parties in which governments become involved and those directly between governments; and with the increase in the number of parties involved in international interchange and activities, the web of interests has grown extremely complex. Frictions arise over business transactions, contracts, customs, understanding (and misunderstanding), trust (and distrust); they also result from efforts by parties whose interests are affected to press governments for expanded benefits or reduction of losses—an example being the protectionist political pressures brought to bear by declining industries. There are also international disputes between governments involving international security and deriving from macro-economic policies.

In the current climate of economic and trade friction, conflicts between individual parties have faded into the background as the dispute between their respective governments has been played up. Many of the "international economic issues" for which solutions are sought between governments are in fact disputes involving technology among a small number of corporations or the result of government efforts to help particular sectors. If we become distracted by disputes between governments, it is easy to lose sight of the real roots of international disputes, such as the complexity of conflicting interests between non-governmental entities whose interests and activities cross national boundaries.

The frictions resulting from interdependence are extremely diverse and complicated, and the parties involved are farflung. The resolution of these conflicts, however, has to be sought largely on a nation-to-nation basis. The only means 4.5 billion people have for seeking solutions is through their 170 or so governments. Each state, moreover, is a forceful political organization sustained by the community of its citizens, and it is a group of these states that in effect controls international society. To put it another way, the deepening of interdependent relations on many levels and the trend toward internationalization of goods, money, corporations, and other economic entities that transcend national boundaries is coming into conflict with the political tendency to give priority to national interests, and this is the cause of all manner of friction among nations.

Thus the burden of public goods required for maintenance of the world's economic order has become far too great to be borne by one nation alone. The need for a system of collective management of the world economy, discussed in the previous section, is a natural outcome of the deepening interdependence among nations. This situation will also intensify, for we are entering an age when the problems of interdependence will have to be resolved through an awareness that the issues of international society are the common concern of all "citizens of one earth." It is, in other words, a time when a new image of international society as a global community must be formed.

The Potential of the Global Community

Through the development of science and technology, the growth of industrial society, and advances in communications, an awareness is taking shape among people on earth that they must work together to find solutions, within the existing physical constraints, to the problems confronting mankind as a whole: environmental pollution, food shortages, damage caused by natural disasters, and the threat of nuclear war. This awareness is potentially a "global community" consciousness or "citizens of one earth" mentality.

Of course, all people on earth do not belong to one huge global community. It is hardly necessary to explain that each individual belongs to a community of people rooted in a geographical territory that is their national land, and that it is these very communities or nation-states that form the basis of international society. It is not likely that this situation will change, at least not in the next 20 or 30 years, although one never knows what may happen 100 years hence. In other words, it is unrealistic, as far as we can see today, to think that the spread of the "citizens of one earth" mentality or consciousness of the global community could fundamentally change the norms and realities of international society in the foreseeable future.

At the same time, apart from the firmly entrenched and discrete communities known as nations, it cannot be denied that international organizations that are not constrained by physical separation are also proliferating as a result of rapid developments in transportation and communications. For example, while there were only about 200 international organizations in existence at the beginning of the 20th century, the figure had risen by 1984 to about 5,000, and these organizations are extremely diverse in form and character. Already many citizens of a particular country are simultaneously members of their national communities and of international agencies or worldwide organizations of all kinds and descriptions. Participation in these myriad organizations renders the national community a relative entity in the minds of its people, and awareness of the global community—a transnational consciousness—is burgeoning.

A global community does not require that the whole globe be embraced by one government or that national boundaries be eliminated; it does not mean a world federation or the abolition of discrete nationalities or nation-states. However, it does transcend the nation, heretofore the largest community, and all national boundaries. Thus, it enables individual citizens of each country in the world to form all kinds of links with people beyond the boundaries of their own nation and, as members of international organizations or groups, to work for the peaceful settlement of international disputes and the establishment of rules and practices for resolving problems. Popular consciousness of the global community will serve to restrain governments from becoming involved in disputes or conflicts for nationalistic reasons.

Japan in a World of Growing Interdependence

Japan's overseas exchange has expanded and is continuing to diversify in every field, and its interconnections with other countries in the world are rapidly deepening. Under the stable postwar system governed by GATT and the IMF, Japan established increasingly interdependent relations with other countries in trade, finance, investment, and other aspects of the economy. In 1970 Japan's dependence on trade (as a proportion of GNP) was about 10 percent for exports and a bit less than 8 percent for imports; by 1984 it had risen to 14 percent for exports and 10 percent for imports.

Moreover, with the deepening interdependence that has accompanied economic growth, the influence of Japan's economy on other countries has considerably increased. As a result, any change in Japan's fiscal or monetary policies, for example, will have a pervasive effect on other national economies—in employment, inflation, and the industrial environment. Likewise, changes in other countries will affect the Japanese economy. As the international financial and capital markets become increasingly integrated through deregulation of domestic markets, Japan's influence will extend—through not only trade but also exchange and interest rates as well as capital transfer—to currency, finance, and every other aspect of other national economies.

The deepening of interdependence in the economy and of relations between Japan and the economies of other countries on the macro-economic level makes policy coordination under a collective management system all the more important.

On the corporate level as well, the international presence of Japanese enterprises is rapidly on the rise. For example, overseas direct investment, in terms of figures reported to the government, rapidly grew in tandem with capital liberalization, from an annual average of around $550 million in the latter half of the 1960s to nearly $2.5 billion in the 1970s and to $10.2 billion by 1984. In addition to overseas production, Japanese corporations are actively engaged in international exchange of investment and technology and in a wide variety of industrial cooperation programs through Original Equipment Manufacturing (OEM) contracts and other arrangements.

At the individual level, the number of Japanese travellers abroad has now risen to over four million annually, twice as many as 10 years ago. The airfare between Tokyo and the West Coast of the United States, for example, is today about one-third of what it was 20 years ago, after adjusting for inflation. In terms of cost at least, the distance has essentially shrunk by two-thirds. People can now cross national boundaries with ease and travel great distances quickly and comfortably, making the world seem much smaller than ever before.

With the increased flow of goods and capital under the system of free trade, rapid developments in the international activities of Japanese corporations, and progress in communications and transportation, as well as with the easing of constraints on international exchange, the distance between Japan and other countries has been drastically reduced, and the Japanese people are already experiencing the sense of a "shrinking" world.

The increased interchange and interdependence between Japan and other countries has provoked friction in many spheres. With the growing impact of Japan's economic presence in the world, friction has arisen over trade and other economic issues, and has grown to encompass the social institutions, customs, practices, and even culture and mode of behavior that characterize Japanese industrial society. Compared with the rapid advances of Japanese products, money, and corporate activities overseas, international exchange of persons and cross-cultural understanding of Japan's society and culture lag far behind, and the lag contributes to friction and misunderstanding. It would appear that Japan, having achieved remarkable economic growth in the postwar period and an exalted position in the world economy, is now being placed at the center of the various disputes and frictions accompanying the deepening of interdependence.

It is probable that both interdependence and friction will continue to increase in international society in the years ahead. Japan, which is a major beneficiary of interdependence, will be in particular need of heightened awareness of the global community. Unfortunately, such consciousness is still weak and insufficient. Today more than ever, it behooves the Japanese government, corporations, and individual citizens to reevaluate Japan's relationship to the world from their respective positions.

B. Japanese Society and the Transformation of World Civilization: Toward a Deepening Internationalization

As outlined above, the world is in the throes of a transformation of industrial society and of the world management system, and the deepening of interdependence is continuing apace. At the same time, in response to the expansion of Western culture, world civilization is changing to a degree unprecedented in history. Japan, having experienced strong growth in the postwar period, exerts strong influence throughout the world. At the same time, frictions have arisen between Japan and many other nations, and Japan often finds itself a target of bitter criticism. It is high time for Japan to find new ways to deepen and improve its relationship with international society. To successfully internationalize, Japan needs to understand the various countries and cultures of the world, as well as to be better understood by them.

Japanese culture is often seen to have features that are so singular as to render internationalization problematic, if not impossible. At the same time, however, it is possible to discern universal values in Japanese culture. These universal values may provide a starting point for bridging cultural gaps and facilitating other countries' understanding of Japan. Today's Japan has to determine the way in which it can best contribute to the new development of world civilization.

1. Japanese Cultural Attributes

Culture is an amalgamation of various factors, including those specific to each nation as a unique combination of ethnic heritage and geographical circumstances: every country in the world has its own characteristic culture. Nevertheless, if a cultural feature peculiar to one country spreads to other countries, is shared by other cultures, or fuses with the characteristics of other countries, this feature can be regarded as universal. Japanese culture, too, shares features with other countries, and this should ease such countries' understanding of Japanese society. Before discussing these "universals," however, let us first review some features that are perhaps peculiar to Japan.

When people from other countries look at Japanese culture, they frequently single out those features which differ from their own culture. Japanese people also tend to feel that Japanese cultural traits are unique. Myriad approaches, many of which are at odds with one another, have been taken to defining these traits. The following discussion of Japanese culture begins by distinguishing between traditional Japanese characteristics and the traits of postwar Japan.

Traditional and Postwar Characteristics of Japanese Culture

In considering Japanese culture, we first have to pay attention to the two formative experiences defining present-day Japan, namely, the defeat in World War II and the rapid economic growth that followed. The characteristics emerging from rapid economic growth are commonly confused with those inherited from Japan's ancient period. Although the attributes of traditional Japan, created over the course of the nation's long history, are unlikely to drastically change, some of those traits which have surfaced during the relatively short postwar period may be more short-lived. Looking toward the 21st century, it is therefore crucial to distinguish the features of traditional Japanese culture from those of postwar Japan.

A distinctive culture emerged from Japan's historical traditions and unusual climatic and geographical circumstances.

First, the natural environment of the Japanese archipelago favored the emergence of a society centering on rice agriculture, in which strong leadership was relatively unimportant. In other words, because the traditional principal industry of Japan—rice cultivation—entailed a great deal of cooperative labor, the Japanese have, since ancient times, been more inclined toward egalitarianism than toward strong leadership. Because this traditional society was characterized by a relatively strong reliance on groups, individual Japanese were very concerned with their reptutation within the group.

For the Japanese, accepting or even recognizing the diverse ethical views of the world's people is not quite second nature. This is partly a result of the tendencies of traditional Japanese society, in particular, the absence of absolute notions of right and wrong. But it cannot be denied that the acceptance of different ethical views is difficult for the people of any nation. Europeans, for example, only established the concept of freedom of religion after hundreds of years of religious wars. In a country like Japan —which is both literally and figuratively "insular," as evidenced by the high degree of commonly shared information—the recognition of ethical diversity may take time. However, Japan's successful internationalization depends on its success in recognizing and comprehending the diverse values of the world's other cultures.

The existence of a shared information network throughout the country, facilitated by Japan's relative isolation as an island, is a second trait of traditional Japanese culture. The characteristics of this network go a long way toward explaining many of Japan's cultural features. For example, this network fostered a type of human relationship that does not rely on detailed explanations to convey meaning. This is related to the way Japanese comprehend human behavior in terms of a duality of *honne* (real intentions) and *tatemae* (official stance). Another example of the influence of this network is the underdeveloped state of contractual thinking in Japan.

The well-known Japanese attention to detail and "bottom-up" pattern of decision-making emerged from this common information network, reinforced by the traditional egalitarianism. The customary attention to detail owed to this traditional recognition of the contributions of all the members of a group working together. As the organizational tendency for superiors to leave most decision-making to their subordinates spread, more attention came to be paid to the ideas of the people in charge of the details of a project rather than the superiors in charge of the whole.

Third, the Japanese emphasis on diligence and frugality was born in the economy of resource scarcity at the end of the seventeenth century. Because of the development of a philosophy stressing the moral virtues of hard work, people were ready to diligently exert themselves without expecting material return. The importance attached to study and learning, symbolized by the Japanese excellence in mass education from the Meiji period on, has similar historical origins.

Fourth, Japan's geographical situation is that of a solitary island, yet it is not so far from the Asian continent that interchange with advanced civilizations was impossible. Its geographic position allowed Japan to incorporate foreign culture and technology while avoiding total intellectual and political domination by foreign powers. Thus, Japanese became "skilled learners," importing what was advantageous.

Unlike these particular traits with their roots in traditional Japanese culture, some of the characteristics of Japanese culture which surfaced during the postwar period may soon change. For example, the so-called lifetime employment system, which came to prevail in large Japanese corporations during the rapid economic growth following World War II, may well not persist into the future. Before the war, few workers had any real job security. Until 1939, there was no law regulating the dismissal of employees, and job mobility was very high. At that time, in Japan as in other Asian nations, families, not corporations, provided for one's welfare. However, in the process of rapid economic growth following the war, traditional communities based on family and regional ties began to break down and lost their hold over the young, who left the countryside seeking new job opportunities in the big cities. Workers' sense of belonging shifted focus from the community to the workplace, which in turn fostered feelings of loyalty to the company. As a result, the quality of these laborers' work improved.

By no means a traditional practice, however, the lifetime employment system is subject to change. The result may be declining company loyalty as well as deterioration in the quality of work.

2. Japanese Characteristics and World Civilization

Having looked at the distinctive features emerging from Japan's own historical tradition and climatic and geographical circumstances, we shall now examine Japanese cultural traits in the context of world civilization.

Western Culture and the Formation of World Civilization

It was not until the 16th-century Age of Discovery that man truly discovered the world, and created a global human society based on economic activities. The advance of the West opened the path to a world united as never before. Western cultural and economic activities gave birth to the world as we know it today, its social order and "common sense" being rooted in Western culture. Most of the languages used around the world are Western languages; the underlying logic of world politics and economics is Western logic. Even the sensibilities of those who manage international enterprises can be said to be Western.

Recently, many Japanese have begun to discuss "internationalism," but the kind of culture most often seen as international is actually Western culture. An example of the way this works comes from international business enterprises. In international enterprises founded in Western nations, many non-Westerners are promoted to managerial positions, but they are expected to deviate little from Westerners in language, logic, and outlook. Even in international enterprises based in Japan, in contrast, non-Japanese (especially Westerners) are not expected, either by their employers or by themselves, to adopt the logic and sensibilities of the Japanese.

The conditions described above might well be considered a disadvantage by many Japanese. However, this situation reflects the historical circumstances of the formation of world civilization, and Japanese must calmly accept that it can hardly be changed overnight.

Incidentally, it is useful to keep in mind that some "Japanese" attributes, the peculiar features of Japanese society and culture, have tended to be exaggerated or slightly distorted when seen in the context of a world civilization centering on Western culture. Since Western civilization provides the language and conceptual framework for understanding the world's cultures, Japanese culture and society may at times look even more peculiar than they actually are. Indeed, it is not only non-Japanese who stress the peculiar (i.e., non-Western) aspects of Japanese culture; Japanese themselves, in search of their own identity, tend to overemphasize these aspects. Singling out the idiosyncracies of Japanese culture has not only become the theoretical principle informing most attempts to "explain" Japanese culture, but has also come to be the standard of behavior for Japanese in international society. In other words, the Japanese tend to face the world donning a mask that exaggerates their "Japaneseness."

Two Aspects of the Japanese Character

Although the image of Japan that prevails in the world may not be entirely inaccurate, it surely is one-sided and distorted. This one-sided image, held by Westerners and Japanese alike, is exemplified by the stereotypical view of the Japanese "organization man." While this term certainly describes some Japanese, it is by no means true of all. To correct this misperception, we shall attempt to introduce a second, less publicized, basic feature of the Japanese personality; first, however, let us consider the Japanese "organization man." In describing these contrasting aspects of the Japanese personality, we do not, of course, mean to imply that all Japanese can be neatly placed into this broad classification scheme.

Organization men have played a crucial role in Japan's industrial development. Deeply loyal to their organizations and highly skilled in group management and human relations, organization men excel at steadfastly pursuing a given goal. They stubbornly cling to their identity, which they narrowly define as the diligent pursuit of a single occupation. In outlook, these men are often strict moralists, and more nationalist than internationalist.

Individuals embodying this personality type created the favorable conditions within Japanese corporations—solidarity, efficiency and devotion to detail—which helped propel Japan to its current prosperity. It should be emphasized, however, that the "organization man" is a second-generation personality type, more concerned with maintaining the status quo than with pursuing new ideas and innovations. Such men have, for the most part, excelled as top managers of large-scale heavy or chemical industries. Although they have not typically contributed new ideas or suggestions for the creation of new industries, their accomplishments were the backbone of Japan's postwar economic development. Tokugawa Ieyasu, who unified Japan in the late Middle Ages and established the basis for maintaining the enduring Tokugawa regime, is a historical figure who exemplifies the virtues of the organization type.

However, a broader perspective on the history of Japan's industrialization reveals an utterly different aspect of the Japanese character, one of adventurousness and strong individualistic leadership. The founders of many corporations, who concern themselves more with new ideas and product innovation, belong to this group. They excel in individual creativity and leadership rather than in human relations or group management. Also, unlike organization men, they are often curious about a wide variety of activities, and more internationalist than parochial in outlook. Many entrepreneurs of the early Meiji period and leaders of the non-basic industries that flourished after World War II represent this personality type. An example among famous historical figures is Oda Nobunaga, who, like Tokugawa Ieyasu, played a major role in the unification of Japan. The genius of Oda was his ability to dismantle and replace the old social order.

The "organization" type is historically personified by farmers and samurai, who were dependent on the land for their livelihood. This attachment to the land, and the provincialism that often accompanies it, is evident in the expression "issho-kenmei," which in current usage means "to do one's best" but literally means "the one place from which you get your livelihood." Similarly, steadfast devotion to one's occupation is revealed in the expressions "kono michi-hitosuji" and "bun o mamoru," which mean, respectively, "devotion to one's profession" and "observing one's proper station." Without a doubt, this personality type closely describes the way most people regard the typical Japanese of today.

In contrast, the second, less familiar personality type, characterized less by provincialism than by internationalism, and less by organizational skills than by innovative ones, is historically exemplified by the Court nobility and by merchants. The frequent emergence on Japan's historical stage of such individuals is often overlooked. In fact, not a few of the Japanese who brought about the country's successful modernization were of this type. Japan's international economic advances are due not only to organization

men, but also to the contributions of these creative and adventurous people.

3. Toward a Deepening Internationalization of Japan

  As we saw above, Japan labors under a disadvantage in today's
civilization owing to the equation of "international" culture with
Western culture. Therefore, Japan's internationalization will be
neither easy nor quick. Furthermore, as we explained, Japanese
need to resign themselves to this reality and seek to adapt to the
widely accepted value standards of the world's people, rather than
pointlessly labeling them inappropriate or wrong. At the same
time, a better appreciation and understanding of the Japanese
and their historical circumstances might hasten the pace at which
Japan has to make great efforts to overcome these obstacles to
internationalization.

  In considering traditional Japanese culture, we should avoid
predetermined or fixed historical views, such as those that rigidly
differentiate East and West, or Japanese and non-Japanese. But
we cannot deny the usefulness of concepts such as the division
between industrial and post-industrial societies in comprehending
human activities.

  The world's developed nations are now in the early stage of
a transformation to a so-called post-industrial society. A shift
from emphasis on physical labor to information and creativity,
in both intellectual and emotional dimensions, is likely to accom-
pany this social change. Japanese organization men will surely
make some contribution, but it is representatives of the entrepreneurial type who will probably come to play a more active role
in this process. Differences between East and West or between
Japan and the outside world will surely be of little significance
compared to the historical watershed between industrial and
post-industrial society.

  Domestically, the revision of Japan's educational, economic,
and social systems is a task of the utmost importance. If these

systems, which sometimes serve to reinforce obsolete Japanese characteristics, are left intact, they could well thwart Japan's transition to the new age of internationalism.

Facing the 21st century, Japanese people today must first correctly understand their own traditional characteristics and then go about making the necessary adjustments in the direction of internationalization. In particular, Japanese should recognize the existence among them of a prototypical character type that is totally different from the stereotypical image of Japanese people: the creative and adventurous personality. More important, after introducing and explaining this personality type to the world, the Japanese must strive to live in accordance with it.

Human beings define themselves through self-perception. An individual tends to behave in accordance with his or her self-image, if it seems valid. If present-day Japanese come to regard the adventurous personality type described above as an appropriate model, perhaps internationalization can be achieved relatively painlessly by switching emphasis from one of the personality types within the traditional culture to another.

To accomplish the more arduous task of contributing to the development of a new world civilization, the Japanese must accept the existence of diverse value systems, and then, like other members of the international community, seek to incorporate their own culture and tradition into the currents of world civilization.

In pursuit of this goal, the Japanese need to rediscover the elements of their traditions that are harmonious with civilization in its present form. Fortunately, the Japanese already have at least one ready-made trait that meets these requirements: the creative and adventurous personality type. The task now is to explain this side of the Japanese personality to the world.

PART II

Japan's Role in and Contribution to the Global Community

A. Basic Approach: Three Courses of Action

As we have observed in Part I, with the emergence of a new industrial society, it is now necessary to create an effective global collective management system. As our international society grows increasingly interdependent, moreover, Japan must strive harder to avoid frictions and disputes as well as to cultivate a deeper sense of solidarity that transcends national boundaries. At the same time, the country's passive posture in world civilization should give way to an active one.

1. Japan as a Principal Participant in the Global Collective Management System: Consciousness of Global Community

The Burden of Global Management

Militarily, as noted in Part I, the international system in the coming decades will continue to be dominated by the bipolar structure built around U.S.-USSR rivalry. The international economy, on the other hand, will probably be directed under a collective management system led by the United States. The system is one in which the major countries collectively share the burden of providing international public goods. Japan is no longer a minor power that can be simply a passive bystander in the collective management system.

The first basic step Japan must take is to become a principal supporter of the collective management system, actively assuming its share of the burden of providing international public goods, as well as working for the maintenance and stability of the international economic system. Such an approach will assure both stable world growth and stable long-term development for Japan.

Under the collective management system in which several countries supply international public goods, a "free ride" problem may arise. For example, a country can benefit from the opening of another's market even though its own remains closed. Clearly, if the supporters of the collective system themselves take this kind of action, the system will collapse. Japan and the other industrialized countries that sustain the system must recognize the crucial importance of their role, and commit themselves to supplying their proper share of international public goods over the long term.

Involvement in the global collective management system means not only assuming a share of this burden but also making the commitment to harmonize national actions with global interests. This will necessitate reform and/or reorganization of political, economic, social, and educational and other domestic institutions as well as skillful adjustments of interests among various sectors within each country. These efforts, necessary as they are, will no doubt be accompanied by considerable friction and turmoil, imposing severe internal strains on the nation. The responsibility of Japanese, in view of their country's position in the world, is to surmount these difficulties on the individual, corporate, and national levels, and to cultivate a global perspective; this entails a shift in emphasis away from short-term national interests and toward long-term global interests. Needless to say, strong political leadership and popular support will be needed if Japan is to successfully shoulder these responsibilities.

Global Community Consciousness

Active participation in the collective management system and assumption of the burden of international public goods will require that nations act, not simply on the basis of narrow national interest, but as flexible coordinators of conflicting interests within and outside their national boundaries and as builders of a better international order. Cooperation and solidarity among nations are necessary in order to maintain and operate the collective management system, and this makes it all the more important that a consciousness of the global community be cultivated among the people of each nation.

Interdependent relations with other countries in trade, finance, corporate activities, and allocation of energy and food resources are indispensable to Japan's stable development. Japan cannot expect to grow or prosper unless the rest of the world grows and prospers. Having benefited vastly from the increasing interdependence of international society, Japan has all the more reason to exert its influence in the formation and maintenance of the international order and, in particular, to set about fostering global community consciousness.

In order to accomplish these objectives, Japan's first task is to strive, on its own initiative, for better understanding of its partner nations as well as to assure that its own actions are correctly understood by other countries. Its initiatives and activities on the international scene will not be accepted unless its actions and aims are adequately explained to other nations. In order to correct misunderstandings and defuse criticism in the international arena, Japan must pay attention to such criticism and make the first move to communicate with others.

Second, Japan must give greater attention to broadening the scope of international exchange and rectifying inequities, keeping the North-South problem in mind. In particular, Japan must be more sensitive to the impact of its official policies and multinational corporate activities on much smaller countries and their industries. So far, Japan has tended to concentrate too much on alleviating the frictions between itself and other industrialized countries such as the United States. Naturally, friendly relations and establishment of smooth international exchange with the advanced nations is important, but it is also increasingly important to take the interests of developing countries and the rest of the world into account. Japan must also pay closer attention to the problem of the abject poverty suffered by an estimated one billion people in the world.

Third, Japan must devote more attention to deterring the outbreak of and facilitating the resolution of disputes that arise as a result of interdependence, as well as of armed conflicts not only global but regional in scale. As interdependence grows, these disputes and conflicts can have a serious impact on the Japanese people, no matter where they take place. Therefore, Japan must redouble its efforts to establish international systems that can resolve disputes before they escalate into larger conflicts. It must also clearly define its role in international security and military affairs, and, based on the goal of international exchange that covers the whole world, including the Eastern bloc, must promote such interdependent relations as will lead to the formation of a global community.

What Japan should and can do now toward the establishment of a global community is to encourage its people to merge with international society. Japan should not be simply a dealer in money and goods, but should become a center for international exchange of people and information. Japan must work harder to make the global community a realistic entity that will benefit other countries and peoples as well as itself.

2. Japan's Economic and Cultural Contributions to the Global Community

The second basic question with which Japan must grapple in determining its role in the world as the 21st century approaches is what kind of presence it will be, and in what fields it will contribute to the welfare of the world.

Japan, having developed remarkably in the postwar period, now holds a leading economic and technological position in the world. However, Japan can never, and should never, become capable of dominating the world through military might. Self-defense is important to Japan, but it is inconceivable that Japan would ever intervene directly to resolve an international conflict using military force.

As a supporter of the collective management system, Japan must not aim to be a hegemonic power preponderant in all fields —economic, military, and international political—but should define its role in the world primarily in terms of economic strength. History gives many examples of countries that were very powerful and influential in the economic field and were respected by other countries. Examples are Venice, a resource-poor trading city-state that flourished from the 13th to the 15th centuries; Holland, a country in similar circumstances that wielded great power in the seventeenth century; and the Sung dynasty of 11th-century China, which owed its influence not to military might but to economic power. These countries also made great contributions to world civilization. Of course, allowances must be made for the international conditions of the times, but these historical lessons suggest a model for what Japan can become in the 21st century, utilizing its economic vitality to help bring about world economic development. By so doing Japan can become both an economic and cultural contributor to the global community.

An "economic and cultural and contributor" might be defined as follows.

Economically, it is a country that has an independent and full capacity for economic growth; strives to maintain and develop a free economic market; and contributes to the development of international economic activities by supplying high quality technologies, commodities, capital, and other management resources and providing markets and a locus for economic activities that are open to all.

It contributes to the management of the international economic system by being a major participant in the collective management system and by shouldering the cost of international public goods (such as the maintenance and development of the free-trade system, economic cooperation, and technology development and transfer). Culturally, it is a country that seeks to enrich its life and culture, as well as to harmonize itself with international society and accept diverse culture, and utilizes its economic strength to promote international cultural exchanges and provide sites for such activities. Politically, it is a country that has self-defense power to sustain a defense-oriented posture, and supports activities safeguarding international security and stability by utilizing its economic strength.

Japan's Role and Contribution under an Open and Free Economic System

In order to be an economic and cultural contributor to the global community, Japan must sustain a sufficiently high economic growth rate. Considering its latent economic strength, Japan ought to be able to maintain such growth in the long run, although this, of course, depends on the international environment. The following points are important if the whole world is to benefit from the vigor of the Japanese economy.

First, as a propelling force in development of the new industrial society and the growth of the world economy, Japan must open up new frontiers in technology and industry. Under the system of collective global management, it must also actively contribute to the establishment of a free and open international economic order. Japan's economy cannot grow without the expansion of world trade and greater imports of energy and raw materials. This is another important factor compelling Japan to devote its utmost efforts to curbing the spread of protectionism and assuming a greater share of the burden in development of the free trade system. It is in Japan's best interest, first, to help improve standards of living around the world by supplying high-quality finished goods and parts as well as by the development and transfer of technology, and, second, to contribute to the development of world industry on the production and supply sides.

Second, as a promising market for foreign-made products, Japan must contribute to the global economy on the demand and consumption sides as well. Japan must work toward expanded equilibrium in the world economy and toward the building of a balanced trade structure, devising an industrial structure that can achieve these goals.

Third, Japan must use its economic surplus to encourage direct overseas investment by Japanese corporations and to extend economic aid to developing countries. Direct investment by corporations will, in particular, have multidimensional effects, such as creation of jobs abroad, the transfer of technology, skills, and management resources, and increased exchange of persons. Expanding interchange and growing interdependence, not only in trade but also in capital transactions, are to Japan's advantage.

3. Japan as an Asian Country: Working for Stability and Regional Cooperation

Japan has deepened its ties with the Asian region, chiefly in economic terms, and has to recognize that it exerts various influences on other Asian countries. If Japan is to play a greater role in the world using its technological and economic vitality, it is crucial that this country acquire more knowledge on Asian affairs as a whole and devote as much effort as possible to furthering stable growth and development in the region.

In the Asian region, interdependence centered around the economy is deepening, and the region's economic potential has drawn close attention from the rest of the world. Regional cooperation among countries of very diverse backgrounds is increasing. How well Japan can fulfill its responsibilities and contribute to the welfare of Asia will be a touchstone in the process of building a worldwide network of cooperative relationships that benefit all nations, and in cultivating global community consciousness.

A Pivot of World Economic Dynamism

The first dimension of Japan's role in Asia is to propagate its economic dynamism throughout the region. The newly industrializing countries (NICs) in Asia, which have enjoyed rapid growth in recent years, are quickly affected by the development of the Japanese economy because of their closely interdependent relationship. The vigor of the Japanese economy pervades these countries as well, stimulating the entire region. The presence of the NICs makes the region too diverse to be described simply in terms of North-South bipolarity, and Japan's role in Asia will be crucial for building a new pattern of relations between North and South.

Recalling how favorable conditions provided by the free trade system during the postwar period helped Japan to achieve rapid economic growth even as a late starter, Japan should do its best to maintain and develop the free trade system and contribute to the region, on the production and supply side through trade, technology, and investment and on the demand side as an open market. Until now, Asian economic development has depended mainly on the American market. The relative sluggishness of that market, however, and the relatively strong position of Japan in the world economy indicate how important it will be for Japan to provide a larger market for products from Asian countries so that the latent vitality of the NICs and other countries in the region can be realized.

Japan must also establish a more closely linked and complementary horizontal and vertical division of labor with industry in Asian countries. To this end, Japan must resolve to actively promote its own industrial adjustment as well as technology and capital transfers for the benefit of its Asian neighbors.

A dynamic Asian economy will mean expanded trade and more investment opportunities in other regions as well. A more extensive web of interdependence will provide new opportunities for development of the global economy and contribute to the development of the entire world. This, of course, is premised on the continuance of the open and free international economic order.

A Contributor to Balanced and Stable Interdependence

Japan's second role in Asia should be the building of stable relations balanced in terms of economic, cultural, and human interchange, with due consideration given to the impact of its actions on other nations.

Other Asian countries have shown increasing interest in Japanese culture and its way of life. However, frictions in the economic realm, which are often blamed on the unbalanced nature of Japan's economic activity, have had a negative impact on cultural relations. Some of the criticisms stem from misunderstandings or one-sided views, but Japan needs to honestly reappraise its role in the region from the perspective of the other Asian countries.

In the fields of human and information exchange, Japan should play a greater role in Asia as a sender and receiver of information and as a forum for exchange of human resources. In addition, Japan must attempt to understand and accept the modern culture of Asia, and to provide a locus for cultural and technological activities in Asia. To the present day, Asian culture has entered Japan by way of the West; there has been little direct opportunity for the other people of Asia to engage in cultural and technological activities in Japan. Japan should reconsider its cultural relations with the rest of Asia. Both the frictions and the growing opportunities for interchange, however, will help to deepen mutual understanding and contribute to heightened consciousness of the global community.

Cooperation for Regional Stability

Japan's third role in Asia is to contribute to stability, growth, and development through economic cooperation, within the context of Asian diversity.

The Asian region includes countries in various stages of development, from those that are already industrialized to those still in the throes of development. Some are richly endowed with natural resources; others depend on imports for their raw materials. The degree of affinity between nations varies widely. The region is diverse not only economically but socially, culturally, ethnically, and in terms of religion. In this pluralistic setting, as economic cooperation grows under the market economy system, economic relations are being given greater priority than military ties. Bilateral interdependence, moreover, has begun to give way to the building of more open, multilateral relationships. As a general rule, it may be said that economic instability in the Asian region is linked to social and political instability, and this can, in turn, escalate to the level of armed conflict.

Japan, which has such an important stake in the stability and prosperity of Asia, must pay close attention to events throughout the Asian region, including the outbreak of localized disputes. It must be tolerant in responding to the requests of its Asian neighbors, and should encourage regional cooperation and stable interdependence in economics, technology, and culture. It is very important that Japan contribute to the political and social stability of each country and to the region as a whole through its economic strength.

The prospect of pan-Pacific cooperation is one that is drawing the attention of every country in the region; as exemplified by the phrase "age of the Pacific," there is much talk of the possibility that an epochal cultural zone may come into being sometime in the future. The economic vitality and dynamism of the region, development achieved through cooperation by countries of varied backgrounds, the potential for the formation of a richly diverse culture, and the heightened interest of the U.S. in the Pacific region are serving to generate momentum toward building a new regional solidarity in the medium and long-term time frame. One of the means through which this can be actualized is an open system of regional cooperation among the Pacific rim countries.*

---

*   Pan-Pacific cooperation has already begun in human and energy resources. Taking a long-term view towards the 21st century, cooperation in energy development will be important. Many energy resources lie untapped in the Pacific region, and a system should be readied that is capable of meeting expected future growth in demand. By convening international conferences engaging in cooperative research and surveys, and by supporting other activities, Japan can contribute significantly to energy development and utilization. Information coordination, especially the consolidation of information infrastructures, will also be extremely important, as explained in Part I, due to rapid developments in information technology. Utilizing its technological and economic power, Japan can make significant contributions to the development of the Pacific region by promoting the establishment of information infrastructures (such as computer networks, data bases, regional communication, broadcasting and earth-resource satellites, and land receiving stations) in Asia and then in the whole region. Japan should make use of these to provide educational and scientific information to the region. In addition, if Japan can act as a broadcasting center through which information from all over the world is dispersed to the Pacific region and vice versa, mutual understanding not only among the nations of the Pacific region but all over the world will be promoted.

B. Japan in the Global Community—Its Role and Responsibilities: A Seven-Part Proposal

In this section we will consider seven areas in which Japan has a significant role to play and in which it can contribute to world progress on the eve of the 21st century. This proposal is based on the three fundamental directions outlined above. Some of the tasks outlined below can perhaps be achieved within a short compass of time, while for others time may be needed to achieve a consensus about implementation. Still others may not bear fruit until the distant future. What is essential, however, is that we begin to come to terms with these tasks at once.

1. Further Expansion of Free Trade: A New Approach to Problems of Industrial Adjustment and Industrial Structure

World trade has expanded far faster than production in the postwar years, and has been a prime factor in the smooth development of the world economy. The greatest impetus behind the upsurge of trade has been the GATT system and its principles of non-discrimination and free trade.

These principles have different repercussions for different nations around the world. This should occasion little surprise: nations vary greatly in levels of economic development; in the types, quantities, and qualities of resources with which they are endowed; and in their fields of expertise. Even within an individual country, various industrial sectors may fare differently in the process of trade. Depending on domestic and international economic conditions, the GATT principles have worked both for and against each country. Nevertheless, most countries of the world have sedulously striven to overcome obstacles, both tariff and non-tariff, and to preserve the basic tenets of free trade. It is this sort of long-term, persistent effort that brought about the reduction of tariff rates following the Kennedy and Tokyo Rounds.

The world economy that was shaped by the principle of free trade is now at an important crossroads. Since the latter half of the 1970s, protectionist pressures have mounted in the developed countries, and various non-tariff barriers to trade have been adopted to protect domestic industries.

The root of this surge of protectionism in the developed countries can be traced to three main problem areas: problems relating to industrial adjustment, issues involving industrial structure, and the general problem of international imbalances. Problems of industrial adjustment are, for instance, unemployment and declining performance in industries that have lost international competitiveness in the course of changes in a nation's industrial structure. Difficulties of this sort mainly produce short-term frictions. By contrast, issues pertaining to industrial structure are long-term ones concerning the type of industrial structure that is suitable or desirable for a given country. The third set of problems of imbalance focus on trade issues such as massive trade surpluses or deficits arising from imbalances between nations. The overwhelming causes of this third types of problem, however, derive from international macro-economic imbalances and will be discussed in detail in the next section.

Meanwhile, the developing countries, which comprise three-fourths of GATT membership, are calling for increased export opportunities, for liberalization of trade in resources and agricultural products (which have been exempt from GATT rules), and for relaxation of import restrictions such as the Multi-Fiber Arrangement (MFA). In order that all the nations of the world may continue to reap its benefits, we must redouble our efforts to expand free trade while trying to iron out the inevitable rough edges. In the following sections, we will consider the problems of industrial adjustment and industrial structure and suggest possible measures for their resolution that will also contribute to the harmonious development of North and South.

(a) Problems Related to Industrial Adjustment

The Causes of the Turn to Protectionism

The merits of free trade are often highlighted by comparing economic conditions of a country with and without trade. The advantages are clear: even a little trade results in improved economic conditions for both partners.

Free trade, however, also engenders numerous difficulties. Those industries in which a country holds a comparative advantage will grow, but weaker industries will see their production curtailed. Thus a shift of production factors from the weaker industries to the comparatively advantaged ones will occur. This process of industrial adjustment, however, becomes problematic when it renders the optimal allocation of production factors difficult. Such distortion is likely to occur when factor prices are inelastic owing to, for example, the downward rigidity of wages, or when transfer of production factors becomes difficult. Ordinarily, labor, land, and capital are relatively fixed and their prices not easily adjusted. If, therefore, inexpensive foreign goods are imported in large quantities, domestic industries producing similar goods often have to wrestle with a slump in profits and rising unemployment. They will naturally seek some sort of trade restrictions, by applying protectionist pressure on their government.

The appearance in recent years of new factors, directly opposed to those that fostered free trade, has rendered protectionism a frequent response to industrial adjustment. The first of these new factors has been a slowing of world economic growth in the wake of the two oil shocks. As a result, fewer growing industries exist to absorb the capital and labor of industries that have lost international competitiveness. This trend has been particularly remarkable in Western Europe. The unemployment rate for all EC countries is now over 10%.

A second factor has been the expansion of trade under the GATT-IMF framework: as trade expands, nations and industries have come to depend more and more on imports, exposing domestic industry to increased competition from abroad. Worldwide, the proportion of domestic demand met by imported goods has risen, from 10% in 1960 to 17% in 1984. Yet as international trade grows, so too does discord. The GATT-inspired multilateral negotiations that reduced many tariff and non-tariff barriers have actually exacerbated the trend toward protectionism by heightening contact between domestic industry and its foreign competitors.

The relative decline of the U.S. economy and concurrent increased competitive power of Japan and the NICs is a third important factor contributing to the rise of protectionist pressures. Since the U.S. has taken the lead in protecting and preserving the free-trade system in the postwar era, a turn toward protectionism on its part threatens to engulf the entire world.

A fourth factor relates to shifts in comparative advantage among nations brought about by rapid technological progress, brisk international capital flows, and exchange rates which have become divorced from the terms of international competition. Comparative advantage is vital in determining the composition of a nation's trade structure, and an unstable comparative advantage picture can complicate the process of industrial adjustment.

Technological advances, however, are altering the structure of comparative advantage by introducing new terms for capital, the quality of labor, and land use. Firms now distribute their productive capacity on a global scale, but land and labor cannot be transferred so easily. Thus the burden of the industrial adjustment that attends shifts in comparative advantage tends to fall on these immobile factors—at least during the transition period until factor price equalization is achieved. In this lies an important cause of the current surge of protectionism. The "cosmopolitan" character of capital and technology clashes with the "local" nature of land and labor; economic internationalism competes with political regionalism.

In other words, in the developed countries, both the cost of industrial adjustment and the frequency with which such adjustments must be made are increasing. As a result, protectionism has come to the fore.

The Economic Consequences of Protectionism

That many countries are resorting to trade restrictions to protect domestic industries results from considerations of policy costs. The cost of import restrictions is distributed widely among consumers, making it hard for an individual consumer of imported goods to grasp the true cost of the restrictions. However, the price the public will have to pay for direct industrial assistance, whether in the form of direct government expenditure or of changes in tax laws, is readily apprehensible. Trade restrictions tend therefore to be politically more acceptable. Moreover, since the benefits to the producer are clear while the cost to the individual consumer is small, trade restrictions, once adopted, tend to be very difficult to do away with.

The Multi-Fiber Arrangement is an excellent example. MFA was adopted by GATT in 1974, but its history goes back to the U.S.-Japan Cotton Accords of 1957. At the time, these accords were little more than voluntary limitations by Japan on textile exports to the United States. Soon, however, the list of exporters covered by the accords grew to include Hong Kong, Taiwan, and Korea, while Western Europe, Canada, and Australia were added to the ranks of importers. In 1961, a "Short-term Agreement on Cotton Products" was concluded based on GATT. This short-term agreement eventually developed into MFA. Originally scheduled to last four years, MFA was renewed in 1978 and expanded in 1982, and in this more restrictive form remains in force to date.

Considering the problems that trade restrictions can engender, it is well that GATT has taken such a strict stance against them. However, the GATT rules are too static to respond effectively to emergency "industrial adjustment" problems at a bilateral level. The spread of "emergency" trade restrictions such as bilateral voluntary limitations on exports, regarded as exceptions to GATT rules, is an example. The very severity of GATT's requirements invites the proliferation of exceptions to its rules. That this should rebound to undermine the original goals of GATT, however, is not at all desirable.

Protectionist measures adopted by developed countries hamper more than just their trade with each other. The developing countries embarking on the path toward industrialization are finding their exports restricted by quotas and other measures. As a result, they will be deprived of opportunities for export and growth, and the difficulties of development will be aggravated.

(b) Problems Concerning Industrial Structure

The Sources of Structural Difficulties

Problems of industrial structure must also be dealt with if free trade is to expand further over the long term. Nations tend to seek as broad an industrial base as they can. They want to develop a diverse structure, embracing agriculture, high technology, iron and steel production, automobile manufacture, etc. Some, operating on the belief that there is a specific set of key industries every nation should possess, attempt to develop all of the key sectors. If each nation strives to do so by imposing limits on foreign imports or inflicts penalizing import duties on competing foreign goods, infringements on free trade are inevitable.

Nations want to possess certain key industries for many reasons, one of which is insurance against future risk. To guard against future crises, nations attempt to achieve self-sufficiency in certain products, or to widen their industrial base, avoiding dependence on the production of a few products alone. A second reason is the desire to create an industrial base, i.e., to secure those industries which are regarded as the basis of a nation's industrial activity. A third reason is that in certain industries the comparative advantage is mobile. Classic examples of these are the so-called "infant industries," and a good contemporary case is high-tech industries. Such industries hold no comparative advantage at the outset, but as experience is gained and production increases, costs fall and they become internationally competitive.

Since the industrial structures of nations are liable to considerable change over the long term, it is clear that the current structure of comparative advantage is not permanently fixed. Nonetheless, it is certain that if the nations of the world continue to impose trade restrictions to foster and maintain certain favored industries, it will be impossible to uphold an efficient world trade system. Similarly, if many nations turn to trade restrictions to bring about a desirable industrial structure, then world trade may lapse into what is known as a "prisoner's dilemma"—no nation will be able to achieve the goals it set for itself at the outset; every nation may find the state of its economy considerably worsened.

The Economic Rationale and Effectiveness of Trade Restrictions

As we have seen, there are many reasons why a country might want to foster a particular industry or network of key industries. However, the economic rationale behind such thinking is dubious. It is also doubtful that trade restrictions are the most appropriate method of resolving structural problems. Let us consider the three justifications listed in the previous section from these perspectives.

Response to Risk   Two issues will be considered here: the problem of self-sufficiency and the question of structural diversification.

The argument for self-sufficiency usually proceeds along the following lines: it is desirable that certain goods be produced internally and that the nation be as self-sufficient in those goods as possible; therefore, import restrictions are appropriate. The problem with this argument is that it does not spell out why self-sufficiency in that particular product is desirable. Even if one decides that a portion of domestic resources should be devoted to the production of a certain product because unforeseen circumstances may make it difficult to import that product, it does not follow that import restrictions are appropriate. To prepare for the worst, it would undoubtedly be far more effective to search out alternative suppliers and to deepen relations with those nations. Agricultural goods are a classic example. Nevertheless, GATT, reflecting the agricultural security policies of developed nations, currently exempts many agricultural products from liberalization. Such measures not only run counter to the fundamental objectives of GATT but also limit the export opportunities of developing nations, many of which depend on agricultural exports.

The argument for diversifying a nation's industrial structure typically takes the following line: if a country's industry specializes in the production of a certain good, fluctuations in the price of or demand for that good can unduly affect the entire economy; to avoid this, some diversity in the structure of domestic industry is necessary. This sort of reasoning is particularly common in developing countries, where the risk of over-specialization is great. Limits on trade are adopted by these countries in order to foster domestic industries through import substitution and to broaden the industrial structure.

Although developing countries are allowed to restrict trade under existing rules, it does not follow that the mere imposition of trade barriers will result in industrial development. It takes more than just production resources such as labor, capital, and land to create an industry. Such intangible resources as technology and management know-how are also indispensable. When these resources are not available domestically, trade restrictions will only make it more difficult to foster industry. Technology transfer, economic assistance, or direct investment from abroad should be preferred to trade restrictions as a means of getting industry off the ground.

Industrial Base   Industries that draw on many other industries for raw materials or parts possess long "coattails." These industries comprise what is known as the "industrial base." In developing countries, where the process of industrialization is just beginning, such industries are needed. And developed countries which plan to center future economic growth around manufacturing also find it necessary to maintain an industrial base. Under GATT rules to guarantee equal opportunity for growth, developing countries are allowed to limit trade in order to foster basic industries. However, as noted above, trade restrictions can do little to secure an industrial base unless all the resources needed to promote those industries are already available in the country. Even when this is the case, it would probably be more effective to seek direct investment or technological transfer.

In developed countries, the concept of industrial base is often interpreted so as to include the protection of declining industries. Economic growth, however, stems from the recurring rise and fall of industries. Protection for declining industries can only nip new industries in the bud. Manufacturing in Europe and the United States is losing competitiveness to Japan and the NICs, but at the same time, new information and service industries are being developed one after the other, particularly in the U.S. In this new wave of economic growth, it may seem economically irrational to erect trade restrictions to protect old manufacturing industries in the belief that they form the industrial base. Except for restrictions imposed to ease the domestic friction accompanying industrial adjustment, there seems little justification for developed countries, moving rapidly to a post-industiral stage, to limit trade in the name of preserving the industrial base, for this will interfere with the development of the world economy. Developed nations should be developing a new industrial base by challenging the frontiers of technology, not by adhering to existing industry.*

One more point should be mentioned here: the difference between the idea of industrial base and the notion that each nation should possess a given set of industries ("one-settism"). Industrial base refers only to the establishment of a basic industrial core. "One-settism" indicates a desire to possess all important industries. The implications of the latter are profound; indeed, if its provisions were perfectly translated into reality, trade, which is premised on the benefits of an international division of labor, could not take place. It is true that nations with large economies possess a very wide range of industries—but this is because internal demand is so great that it cannot be met entirely by imports, even for products in which the country does not hold a comparative advantage. This is a different matter, however, from the erection of trade barriers in an attempt to cultivate a full set of industries.

Future Comparative Advantage   The discussion of future comparative advantage will be illustrated by two examples: infant industries and high technology.

Infant industries are those which, although confronted by strong foreign competition and comparatively weak at the outset, seem destined to develop a strong comparative advantage in the future. As they gain experience and are able to increase production, they will amass technology and develop a skilled pool of labor. Again, it is in the developing countries that the need to develop such industries is most pressing. Much of the issue here overlaps with the problem of developing an industrial base. From an economic standpoint, infant industries should be fostered only when the social costs incurred during the initial development stage can be made up by social benefits derived later. Developing countries are allowed under GATT to impose trade restrictions

---

* A member of the Round Table expressed the opinion that in view of the current situation, in which the developed countries of Europe and America are gradually losing their industrial bases because of competition from Japan and other countries, the spread of opposition to free trade can scarcely be avoided. In the future, Japan and other countries which have rapidly expanding exports should correct their over-reliance on exports.

for this purpose, just as they are allowed to do so to develop an industrial base.

Yet because in many developing countries the industrial sector as a whole is underdeveloped, it is exceedingly difficult to single out a specific industry for special attention. Japan, the United States, the European Community, and the other developed nations should do their utmost to support economic development in the developing countries by opening markets and providing economic assistance and technology.

When it comes to high-tech industries, the number of producers is quite small. Instead of being predetermined at the outset, comparative advantage often changes with the amount invested in research and development and production experience. In such industries, whoever pioneers production will have a decisive influence on future patterns of trade. And because of the great "dynamic economies of scale" in both accumulated experience and research and development expenditures, it is very difficult for others to catch up. The result is a tendency toward monopoly or oligopoly in high-tech markets.

Since the future size of the market is unknown, many nations look to high-tech industries in the hope of sustained high growth. In order to break international monopolies or to secure future growth opportunities, nations which have lagged in the high-tech area may restrict trade and manipulate domestic demand to gain leverage with which to nurture such industries. Such protection for domestic markets may be economically rational for a single nation. However, if no limits are imposed on these kinds of protective measures, they threaten to spread across the globe. In most cases, moreover, it is the developed countries which have the necessary infrastructure for development of high-tech industries. Since these countries already have well-developed economic foundations, trade restrictions on their side cannot be justified by a need to promote domestic industrial development.

In short, in the high-tech sector as well, trade restrictions ought not to be the lever for industrial growth. Rather, policies addressing structural problems (for instance, increased support for research and development) should be the key.

If each country formulates different policies to foster industry, there is a danger that the terms of competition may become unbalanced. Thus an international consensus is needed to ensure that individual national policies be made clear to all. Furthermore, to avoid the squandering of resources that results if nations oversubsidize research and development for policy reasons, measures to encourage joint development should be enacted. In any case, a new set of international rules or revisions of existing regulations may be needed to ensure that nations do not resort to trade restrictions in the high-tech sector.

For the Further Growth of Free Trade

The GATT system was intended to prevent the kind of disintegration into economic blocks and race to erect tariffs that caused a shrinkage of the world economy during the Great Depression of the 1930s. Its principles were designed to build a system of trade that is non-discriminatory and free. The reason that the system of free trade has, through its ups and downs, been supported to this day lies, at least in part, in the fervent desire of the nations of the world to avoid the sort of spiral of revenge that once brought the world economy to its knees.

Forty years of economic development have passed since the end of World War II and the inauguration of GATT, and problems have begun to appear to which the current GATT system cannot adequately respond. Protectionism has reared its head in many nations, and the principles of free trade are being closely scrutinized. To halt the spread of protectionism and to ensure that the nations of the world continue to reap the benefits of the international division of labor stimulated by free trade, some sort of international consensus is necessary. The following points constitute our proposal.

1.   In order to provide equal export and growth opportunities for developing countries, liberalization of resources and agricultural products—many of which are still treated as exceptions under GATT—is called for. The developed countries should adopt a wider perspective and apply themselves to domestic industrial adjustment and the liberalization of trade in agriculture and similar areas. Trade restrictions erected by developing countries to encourage structural diversification or the development of an industrial base should be tolerated within limits. However, such trade restrictions alone are counterproductive. The de-

veloped countries should actively participate in the economic growth of the developing world through direct investment, technological transfer, and economic assistance.

2. The existing rules that allow trade restrictions to be imposed for emergency industrial adjustment should be revised. As noted above, GATT allows import restrictions to protect domestic industry from sudden surges in imports, but only under strict regulation. These regulations do not allow import restrictions targeted against a specific country, nor do they necessarily allow them to be managed flexibly. For these reasons and others, the current GATT rules do not provide for sufficient leeway in exercising import restrictions. The result is that an increasing number of trade restrictions are being implemented outside the bounds of GATT. If this situation is left unattended, trust in GATT may be shaken and the structure of free trade weakened. New safeguards will be needed. Of course, to prevent trade restrictions from proliferating and becoming permanent, nations undergoing industrial adjustment should be obliged to cooperate in policy formulation, and measures should be devised to ensure that trade restrictions are withdrawn in a timely fashion. The fundamental policy vis-à-vis declining industries in developing countries should be to encourage domestic industrial adjustment. Long-term trade restrictions for the preservation of such industries should not receive international recognition.

3. In the high-technology sector, new initiatives are necessary to allow full rein to the competitive principle and to achieve efficient production on a global scale. Since few countries have much experience in the field, specific guidelines may be difficult.

However, the future promise of high technology is such that each nation must be free to compete in developing these industries. Proliferation of trade restrictions in this field must be avoided at all cost. If we are committed to providing each nation with equal opportunity for growth and enrichment, we should also be committed to constructing a new international order that will allow this without resorting to trade restrictions. Standards are needed to guarantee that each country's policies are made clear to all. This will help ensure that national policies fostering specific industries do not vary greatly and is also important in light of the desirability of equalizing the terms of competition.

Also, since nations are individually pouring vast amounts of capital into the high-tech field in search of high future growth and increased income, a framework to encourage joint research and development should be devised to promote efficient use of these funds.

By way of conclusion, a few words on Japan's role in these areas are in order. Japan is one of the countries that has reaped the greatest benefits from free trade, and Japan's support for free trade in the years ahead will be important for the other countries of the world. Since the growth of the Japanese economy will depend on the expansion of world trade, Japan should do as the United States did in the decades after World War II and take the lead in opening and liberalizing its own markets. Fully one-tenth of the world's GNP is produced in Japan, and it has become not only an important manufacturing base for the world but also a valuable market. Commensurate with its position, Japan should actively encourage domestic industrial adjustment and provide markets for foreign goods. Such an effort will enable Japan to play a leading role in furthering the development of free trade, and this in turn will rebound to the profit of the Japanese economy over the long run.

In the preceding pages we have considered some of the measures that are necessary for the further expansion of trade. But we should be reminded that the world economy is not held together by trade alone. The macro-economic policies of the nations of the world (at least the developed countries) are closely linked, and an active transnational flow of capital, technology, and even people takes place on a daily basis. As a result, currency exchange rates, for example, have come to reflect more the macro-economic policies of various nations than economic rationality. Also, because direct investment and technology transfer are not taking place on the scale they should, the potential comparative advantage of developing countries is not being fully realized. These sorts of difficulties show up as distortions in trade.

A solution to these trade distortions, therefore, cannot be attained merely by maintaining an orderly system of trade. In fact, many trade distortions arise because non-trade areas are not subject to the same powerful, rationalizing discourse as is trade in goods. If we aim to construct a truly global community, we

must also construct a common world order that is based on shared
values and shared appreciation of the problems that affect international intercourse.*

2. Toward Structural Policy Coordination: Correcting International Macro-Imbalances

The international macro-economic system faces a period of
major changes. The basic reason for this is that the flexible exchange rate system adopted in 1973 has failed to stabilize the
world economy, and macro-economic structures in different
countries have drastically diversified. Interdependence caused
by the expansion of trade and the dramatic upsurge in international capital flows are important factors behind this situation.

The present section will discuss possible means of rectifying
international macro-economic imbalances. It will consider the
future direction of the international exchange system and explore

---

* The concept of "fair trade" was also discussed. Views varied widely over what
should be considered fair for whom and who should give in to whom in the name
of fairness. Opinion was split over whether fair trade should be regarded as a
concept in harmony with or contradictory to the idea of free trade. Members held
differing opinions about the proposal that we should seek to harmonize the systems
of each country so that the people of the world come to understand and share the
same customs and national institutions in order to further the growth of free trade.

With regard to the general causes of protectionism, one member commented
that in the past excessive trade surpluses were reduced by investing part of the
surplus overseas, or in economic cooperation. The problem was also met by
increased domestic demand for investment in social capital and raising the living
standards of the nation's people. Imports were also increased, armaments improved,
and large numbers of foreign immigrants allowed in. All of these entailed large
expenditures vis-à-vis the outside world. Nineteenth century England and the
United States, in this century, each followed this course and contributed greatly to
the recovery of world economic balance. In the future, too, nations holding large
trade surpluses should follow this lead. Although it may prove impossible to carry
out all of these tasks, Japan should at the very least open its markets, even if this
will cause painfully difficult industrial adjustment. As will be discussed below,
domestic demand must be increased, foreign travel encouraged, and economic
cooperation expanded. Also, in order to spur direct investment in developing
countries, policies should be devised that will cover some of the risks of investment.

the question of what monetary and financial systems should be adopted. Finally, Japan's role in the international community will be examined.

(a) Policy Options

Policy options available for rectifying international economic imbalances include the following:

1) manipulating the money supply through monetary or fiscal policy (a fixed-rate system);
2) leaving the adjustment to the free fluctuation of the exchange rate (a floating-rate system);
3) partial restraints on trade or external capital flows; and
4) multilateral policy coordination.

Needless to say, whatever system is chosen, self-discipline in domestic macro-economic policy is essential for the successful rectification of international macro-economic imbalances.

Fixed Exchange Rates

Experience under the Bretton Woods system has shown that fixed exchange rate systems are fraught with difficulties. First, fixed rates entail a loss of autonomy in domestic economic policy-making. Financial authorities in each country are forced to adjust the domestic currency supply in response to changes in international transactions. Inevitably, their decisions with regard to money supply matters are based on consideration of the international economic balance rather than on domestic policy considerations. Autonomy in fiscal policy-making would also be impossible, since fiscal policy decisions affect the balance of domestic savings and investment.

A second problem with fixed rates is that financial authorities would probably have great difficulty maintaining the prescribed exchange rates in today's circumstances. World trade has expanded greatly, and the volume of capital transactions has increased tremendously with financial liberalization and the growth of capital markets. In Japan alone, trade has almost tripled in the past decade, while long-term capital transactions volume has increased more than tenfold. Furthermore, in contrast to the postwar period of relatively stable economic development, the present growth of the world economy is highly uneven, and international capital flows have become fluid in the extreme. In light of these realities, it seems highly unlikely that financial authorities could support fixed exchange rates over the long run.

Floating Rates

The second option is to allow exchange rates to float freely with market forces. The current situation, however, proves that a system of floating exchange rates alone is incapable of eradicating the vast range of existing imbalances. When the floating rate system was adopted in 1973, there were high hopes that it would function to correct current account imbalances by causing currencies to rise and fall in step with the economic conditions in each country. It was also hoped that this would aid the recovery of domestic autonomy in determining economic policy. In reality, however, the rapid increase of international capital flows, brought about by the relaxation of restrictions on capital transactions and other factors, created even greater global interdependence on the macro-economic level. This growing interdependence has created new difficulties. For one, capital movements, rather than trade, have come to be the dominant force in determining exchange rates.

Since exchange rates no longer primarily reflect movements in current accounts or short- and mid-term economic fundamentals, the system of floating exchange rates has ceased to function as an autonomous stabilizer. As a result, macro-economic imbalances have, contrary to expectations, expanded.

Partial Restraints on Trade or External Capital Flows

The third option is to confront the problem directly through restrictions on trade or capital flows. In the current situation, however, trade restrictions alone can do little, if anything, to rectify macro-economic imbalances.

Under floating rates, disequilibrium in a country's current accounts means that a gap exists between production and consumption in the domestic economy (i.e., there is a gap between domestic savings and investment). As long as sources of macro-economic imbalance remain in the domestic economy, restrictions on trade will be generally ineffective at balancing current accounts.

In today's economic environment, if a country imposed restraints on exports, the only result would be a drop in the value of the country's currency: there would be little correction of the country's current account balance. Similarly, controls placed on capital flows would only result in a loss of the economic efficiency enjoyed under a system of free financial transactions.

The international flow of capital has become economically significant in and of itself. It can adjust shortages or surpluses of capital in each country, and alter the balance of saving and investment according to the country's level of industrial and economic development. In developing countries, capital (i.e., savings) tends to be relatively scarce, so investments are generally financed by capital imports. Attempts to regulate the flow of capital by artificial means may well distort the international supply of and demand for capital. If Japan, for example, which has one of the world's highest savings rates, were to restrict trade or capital flows, it would be abandoning its role as a supplier of international capital, and the result would be shortages of capital in some countries.

The three options discussed above, then, are not adequate solutions for the current situation. To overcome today's problems, it is necessary for countries to coordinate their domestic monetary and fiscal policies in such a way that the value of their currencies still reflects their fundamental economic conditions. Self-discipline in domestic macro-economic policy is a major premise for successful policy coordination.

(b) Adjustments through Policy Coordination

There are two approaches to policy coordination for the rectification of international macro-economic imbalances. The first is cooperative intervention in exchange markets, and the second is coordination of monetary and fiscal policy among nations.

Coordinated Intervention in International Exchange Markets

As noted above, past experience proves the necessity of intervening in exchange markets in order to keep current account imbalances within allowable ranges. Intervention can be approached in two different ways: the first is to establish target zones which set acceptable ranges for exchange rate fluctuations;

the second is the type of intervention exemplified by the Group of Five, which would manage rates without setting specific target values. Such intervention can be effective when foreign currency imbalances stem from specific short-term circumstances.

It should be stressed, however, that the expansion of world capital markets has made it difficult to maintain artificial controls on foreign exchange markets over the long term. Controlled intervention presents no problems so long as it is directed at enhancing market trends or curbing exchange rate volatility. Certain types of intervention, however, may give rise to un-warranted expectations about market trends, thus stimulating speculative capital flows and actually increasing market insta-bility. Attempts to keep exchange rates at a certain level often invite disastrous results in a context of free and active capital flows. For example, even under a target-zone system, international disequilibria might grow to the point where they could no longer be corrected within the target zone, and a currency might become stuck at the top or bottom end of the zone. This might lead to large-scale speculative transfers of capital in expectation of the establishment of a new target zone, and cause a loss of confidence in the currency. Thus, even though intervention is necessary in order to avoid overly large fluctuations in exchange rates, macro-economic policies must also be coordinated in order to maintain the efficiency of intervention in the long run.

International Coordination of Monetary and Fiscal Policies

The fiscal and monetary policies of different countries should be coordinated to adjust macro-economic structure (savings-investment balance) and rectify international macro-economic imbalances. This will also make possible well-organized inter-vention in exchange markets.

In Japan, for example, the balance between savings and invest-ment is heavily tilted toward savings. This corresponds to Japan's huge surplus in current accounts and its deficit in capital accounts. Expansion of consumption will be needed to restore the balance between savings and investment, but a more comprehensive program of stimulation of domestic demand through encouraging private fixed investments, or increasing public investment, must also be considered.

Capital and public investment over the coming decades should emphasize consolidation of the living environment through investment in housing and the like and the development of the infrastructure necessary for an information-based society. These will give Japanese a more affluent lifestyle and establish a basis for the new post-industrial society. Japan's laying of the groundwork for the creation of an information-based society may itself be considered a contribution to world progress. In addition, it will result in a greater balance between savings and investment and help to restore the balance of trade.

The mechanisms that spur excess savings will also need to be adjusted. The current tax system, for example, needs revamping.

It is easy enough to point to the mammoth U.S. deficit as the cause of present macro-economic imbalances, but simply pointing this out contributes little to finding an actual solution to the problem. Japan should first tackle those problems that are within its control.

If handled appropriately, a system of coordinated intervention and coordination in fiscal and monetary policies would lead to a system of multiple reserve currencies. Such a system would parcel the responsibility for the international business cycle out among several countries, enhancing the stability of the world economy. If a country has sufficient economic, political, or military strength, there may arise a general demand for that country's currency to become an international or reserve currency. Internationalization of the yen in this way is desirable in that it would preserve overseas capital and expand the available range of reserve currencies. Many problems would arise if the yen were made an international currency without regard for market factors; however, any regulations or structural obstacles that prevent demand for yen from being adequately met should be eliminated. Offshore financial markets in Japan should also be expanded.

The use of multiple international currencies might mean that fluctuations in international exchange rates would cause even greater instability in the world economy, and possibly even fragmentation into regional currency blocks. International policy coordination is needed to avoid this sort of risk. Or, to put it another way, policy coordination might lead naturally to a system of multiple international currencies.

(c) Successful Policy Coordination

The growing number of macro-economic links between nations means that self-discipline and international cooperation in fiscal and monetary policy will be indispensable components of any program to correct international macro-economic imbalances. It is, however, far more difficult to coordinate policy among nations than it is to manage the macro-economic policy of a single country. In many cases, steps necessary for achieving international balance may conflict with domestic policy goals with respect to business cycles, for example. If they hold fast to internationally established policy, nations can expect to face a good deal of domestic criticism. However, if international macro-economic imbalances are to be corrected, and the ill effects of exchange rate fluctuations are to be lessened, some sort of policy coordination cannot be avoided. Successful policy coordination by the major industrialized nations is the key that will determine whether or not a system of collective management of the international economy is possible.

What follows is an examination of three conditions necessary for successful policy coordination. These are: (1) a shared perception of the economic situation and agreement on policy goals; (2) increasing policy options; and (3) coordination of systems.

(1) Shared Perception of the Economic Situation and Agreement on Policy Goals

The chances of successful policy coordination would be close to nil if, say, an imbalance arose in the current accounts of two countries, and each country had different perceptions of the cause of the imbalance. Policy coordination will, thus, be extremely difficult if the nations involved do not share a common conception of the economic situation.

Even if a common perception of the economic situation can be reached, policy coordination will still be difficult without agreement on policy aims. Should stress be placed on the international balance of payments? Or should balanced budgets be emphasized? Is full employment to be the goal? Price stabilization? Or something else?

Of course, domestic political concerns will influence any

attempt to pursue such policy aims. Given, however, that Japan's economy can remain sound only if Japan works in harmony with the world economy, both the government and the people must give priority to policy coordination, and must be prepared to accept a certain amount of domestic political conflict.

(2) Increasing Policy Options

Although policy coordination may curb the autonomy of individual nations, that is a price that must be paid in order to enjoy the advantages of coordination. It will, therefore, be worthwhile to seek out a wider range of policy tools that give more leeway to governments. For example, Japan has already relaxed its monetary policy, and its financial situation has made fiscal policies difficult to manipulate. In light of this, some believe that domestic demand should be stimulated by modifying existing regulations affecting land, housing, and taxation alone.

Broadening the range of policy options means adding other policies to the standard monetary and fiscal responses. It adds another degree of freedom to policy choice.

(3) Coordination of Systems

The economic policy-making systems of different countries must also be made more similar. One possibility would be to coordinate tax provisions affecting savings and investment rates. Moreover, since differences in social welfare systems, direct and indirect taxation schemes, and financial and capital market regulations can also give rise to macro-economic disequilibrium, it may be desirable to set up a forum to consider how to prevent structural differences and varying regulations from hampering policy coordination. Where possible, uniform international rules should be established. Of course, this kind of standardization is extremely difficult, since the systems and regulations of each nation are based on social conditions and aims particular to it. Achieving domestic and international economic balance is difficult in many ways. If stress on international equilibrium undermines domestic policy aims, the system itself should be reevaluated and changed so that it can function effectively both externally and internally.

To achieve these goals, a new international economic order for policy coordination should be encouraged. Establishing a regular scheme for the exchange of opinions on macro-economic policy planning might be a step in this direction. Japan has a potentially large role to play in this process; it should act as a leader of the effort, and not merely as a passive observer.

It is imperative that Japan be fully aware of its economic position and of the impact of its actions on the world. Japan's economic vitality is great, even compared with the other developed nations, and it is generally acknowledged that it will not lose this position in the immediate future. Yet, if Japan gives priority solely to its own domestic needs, it will surely be unable to solicit cooperation from other nations. Macro-economic policy coordination is a first step toward a system of collective management of the international economy, and Japan must act as a leader in this effort.

3. Encouraging Mutually Beneficial Direct Investment: Corporate Contributions to Economic and Technological Progress

The past 20 years of activity by Japanese corporations in Southeast Asia, in Central and South America, and of course in the West testifies eloquently to the degree of internationalization they have attained. No one can deny that the business world —corporations in particular—has been the most consistent promoter of internationalization. The term itself, formerly referring simply to the existence of trade relations, has come to signify a much more extensive involvement with foreign countries in the form of direct investment.

Japan's direct overseas investment in recent years has increased at a higher rate than that of other major countries. This results not only from a growing surplus of savings at the macro level, but also from the rapid accumulation of managerial resources by Japanese firms. This trend will become more marked as we approach the 21st century.

Direct investment allows superior management resources to be widely and deeply infused into a foreign community. In addition to being an extremely valuable contribution to technological and economic progress in the host country, it also deepens interdependence and promotes mutual understanding between the investing country and the host country. However, direct investment calls for broader human exchange than movements of capital or technology alone. It necessitates communication on various fronts: not only between labor and capital, but also with local business partners and the surrounding society at large.

In the subsequent sections, we will consider the significance and potential contributions of overseas direct investment. Several suggestions will then be presented in the hope that they may help to smooth the process of direct investment and increase its economic benefits.

(a) The Economic Significance of Direct Investment

The international movement of production factors takes a variety of forms. In some cases, as in the purchase of foreign securities or overseas loans, only capital is involved in the flow. At other times, the flow of capital may be accompanied by a comprehensive transfer of managerial resources. ("Managerial resources" refers especially to knowledge and experience in production, personnel management, procurement of materials, sales, capital acquisition, etc.) In still other instances, technology alone, managers alone, or some combination of the two may be transferred. In general, the significance of direct investment can be measured by the impact a comprehensive transfer of managerial resources will have.

The benefits for the investing firm of direct overseas investment include: 1) securing markets in the host country; 2) lowered production costs because of the availability of inexpensive supplies of labor and raw materials; 3) the possibility of "indirect" export of goods and services (e.g. financial, insurance, and commercial services) that cannot be exported directly; and 4) benefits gained from preferential policies by the host country. Basically, the decision to internationalize involves the same motives that lie behind a firm's domestic growth policy.

Direct investment, however, seems a particularly opportune vehicle for a firm's internationalization. Direct investment allows a distribution of managerial resources that takes into account future international comparative advantage and also allows firms to avoid trade friction from the start.*

Considered at the national level, the decision as to which managerial resources should be transferred to achieve an economically optimal result depends on the configurations of production factors possessed by the two countries involved. If all countries of the world possessed an identical production/technological structure, then utility would be maximized basically by allowing free trade or the free flow of capital. If an inadequate stock of production technology is the only problem, then technology transfer should suffice. Postwar Japan, which achieved high growth by importing technology rather than by receiving direct foreign investment, is one example of the efficacy of this pattern. It should be noted, however, that Japan was blessed with an abundance of capital by virtue of its high savings rate, a budgetary surplus resulting from its strict fiscal policy, and a highly skilled work force. It is doubtful that other countries will be able to achieve similar success by simply copying Japan's example: the preconditions behind Japan's success must also be fulfilled.

The significance of direct investment is that the entire complex of managerial resources is transferred. Its function and significance lie in its ability to bring about wide-ranging improvements in production and managerial technology at a single stroke.

Contributions to Local Progress through Direct Investment

The vast expansion of Japanese direct investment in recent years was predicated on the rapid quantitative and qualitative growth of Japan's managerial resources.

Even with efforts to reduce excess saving and increase consumption, the saving surplus is likely to persist at least until the begin-

---

* A member pointed out that direct investment in other countries may contribute to the "de-industrialization" of Japan. However, no consensus could be reached on the meaning of de-industrialization or on the types of problems it might cause. For example, when the effects of de-industrialization on employment were discussed, it was pointed out that new industries in the service sector and elsewhere may be able to make up for the employment lost in manufacturing industries, thus partially alleviating the severity of the unemployment problem. It was also argued that the vitality of Japan's manufacturing sector will be maintained.

ning of the next century, by which time the aging of society may affect the savings rate. The allocation of this precious surplus between domestic and overseas investment is a matter of great importance. Direct investment in promising young countries will rank equally with improvements in social infrastructure through domestic investment as a valuable source of revenue to finance future consumption. If Japanese firms are to establish themselves firmly in international society over the long run, they cannot rely merely on trade, but must redouble their effects at direct investment.

Expanding direct overseas investment as a response to the rising demand for capital and managerial resources is one of the most significant steps Japan could take, not only for itself, but for the entire world. Not only will direct investment aid the general economic development of the recipient country; it will give rise to other benefits as well.

First, there are various spin-off effects: expanded employment opportunities, increased tax revenues for the host government, and higher sales for the investing firm through the acquisition of local raw and manufactured goods. Secondly, direct investment can raise workers' skills, transfer marketing and administrative know-how, and contribute to the growth of local industry. Through direct investment the managerial resources built up by corporations in the home country can be transmitted to local managers and employees, thus increasing the production efficiency of the host country.

If Japanese direct investment is to contribute to long-term growth of the host countries, special emphasis must be placed on the second type of benefit. Direct investment in the form of transfers of technology and skills will become increasingly important.

(b) Direct Investment as a Means of Transmitting Superior Skills and Technologies

Transnational movement of superior production technologies and management skills will contribute significantly to the world economy. It is desirable, however, that these skills and technologies be widely diffused throughout the economy of the host country rather than remaining within the confines of the firm. What needs to be emphasized here is that direct investment is a much better way of transferring skills and technologies than methods such as the exchange of scientific literature, the acquisition of patents, or the introduction of know-how. This is because technology transfer stimulated by direct investment takes place through the actual movement of people.

Interpersonal contact is one of the most effective ways to transmit skills and technologies. Of course, manuals and other educational materials are also valuable; but since the finer details of many skills cannot be specified or explained in manuals, it is often necessary that they be demonstrated by someone who has mastered them. For example, the delicate control operations performed by a skilled operator at an automated factory can only be mastered through hands-on experience at the workplace; imitation of a trained teacher is indispensable to mastering the technique. Examples of skills and technologies that are best transmitted by personal contact are not limited to those related to direct investment: history is replete with many other examples.

The organization of the firm and its incentive system can also have a major impact on the acquisition of skills. All skills have aspects which cannot easily be specified in manuals, and it is essential that the firm be able to evaluate how well an employee has grasped such intangibles. Few things are more damaging to morale than the judging of employees solely on the basis of whether or not they can perform certain specified tasks. Establishing incentives to stimulate employee creativity and ingenuity is an important part of managerial technique. By introducing superior management concepts, improved corporate organization, and better incentive systems, direct investment can make a significant contribution to the host country.

There is a sequence that must be followed in the acquisition of a new technology. Especially in an industrial setting, almost all new technologies build on old ones. Before earlier technologies have been absorbed, no newer ones can be mastered. An example is the new "mechatronics." For this sort of technology to take root, the society must already have attained a certain level of skill with traditional metal processing machinery and possess the technologies needed for the production, maintenance, and repair of application machinery. A certain sequence must, therefore, be observed in selecting the industries and technologies that are most appropriate for the host country's level of economic development. So that direct investment can proceed smoothly and successfully, Japan should cooperate in providing peripheral technologies and in improving the host country's socioeconomic base.

Direct investment is a superior method of transferring "living" skills and technologies to other (especially developing) countries through the transfer of human and material resources. Japanese corporations need to realize that direct investment is a superior form of private-sector economic cooperation, and to develop it in a manner that minimizes conflict.

(c) Promoting Mutually Beneficial Direct Investment

As described above, direct investment is effective both in putting Japan's economic vitality to work in the world and in contributing to the development of the host country. From the standpoint of the firm, however, direct investment is just one of a number of methods of achieving optimal utilization of its managerial resources. Since it is the prospect of profit that induces corporate managers to take risks, it is only natural that the profit motive is the most important decision-making criterion. It must be recognized, though, that the pursuit of short-term profits may jeopardize the long-term profitability of the firm.

Direct investment, unlike investment in securities and the like, requires that capital be tied up for an extended period of time. For direct investment to remain fruitful over the long run, close relations must be maintained with local employees, firms, and local society, and the investing firm must strive to contribute to the development of the host country. Care should be taken lest the locals feel that foreign ways are being imposed on them. If Japanese enterprises can blend into the local socioeconomic system and become an indispensable part of local society, then the host government will be much less likely to take measures prejudicial to the Japanese firms, because such measures would hurt the local economy as well. Negligence in such efforts will not only increase the risk of jeopardizing the investment but will draw a dark cloud over all of the firm's activities, including exports from Japan. What guidelines, then, should a firm adopt that will contribute to the long-term development of the host country?

First, the economic benefits of direct investment must be appropriately distributed between the firm and the host country. This does not imply that there is any rigid rule about how the benefits should be divided; if done forcibly, such division may subject the firm to unreasonable risks. In general, the most effective means of ensuring that corporate profits flow not only to Japan but also into the local society include joint ventures, stock offerings (after a certain period) incorporating local capital into the firm, and local reinvestment of profits.

Second, steps should be taken to promote the transfer of production skills and technologies. For example, importance should be attached to the development of a broad group of "core" technicians in the developing countries, who will be able to digest and utilize imported technologies on their own to a certain extent. And since Japan will be a major source of new technologies, a deeper understanding of Japan—its general technological level, its society, its outlook, etc.—will likely be important. Thus, a system under which engineers from developing countries can study and be trained in Japan should be set up. Although already in effect to some extent, this system merits much greater attention.

The transfer of work processes that mesh with the host country's level of development will be conducive to its long-term economic well-being. Direct investment involving the transfer of only a few processes that do not fit local labor or technological requirements not only will stand in the way of an efficient distribution of resources, but can hardly bring about a complete diffusion of technologies. Such investment can scarcely be welcomed by the host country. In contrast, direct investment congruent with the level of development of production factors in the host country, including labor and technology, will enhance the international division of labor and facilitate the construction of industrial structures appropriate for each country.

A third imperative for the Japanese firm is movement towards a unified structure of the labor force in the parent company and its local subsidiaries. For example, decision-making should be shared by the Japanese parent company with its local subsidiary. It is especially important that local employees have a chance to participate. To this end, local employees with good management and administrative skills should be trained and promoted. The promotion track should be clearly defined and should lead into the parent company itself. In the long run, the personnel system of the parent company should be changed to accommodate non-Japanese nationals. If Japanese dominate all the key positions and if promotion into the parent company is impossible, local employees with superior management skills can hardly be expected to remain with the company for long. To facilitate communication between the parent company and its local subsidiary, it is also important for the parent company to send abroad workers who are familiar with the local situation in the host country.

Fourth, firms advancing into overseas markets must not disrupt the local social order. These firms often possess strong influence, even overwhelming dominance, in local markets, especially in developing countries. Such firms have on occasion used their positions to reap excessive profits or to engage in such ruthless competition for market share that the development of local industries was stifled. These are fundamentally matters that can be dealt with by the host country through capital import or anti-monopoly policies, but the investing firms themselves should also be mindful of such problems.*

Finally, the firm and its managers should participate in local events and assist in charitable activities (contributing both time and money) in order to maintain a general level of exchange between the firm and the indigenous population.

Necessary Public Measures

Internationalization and direct investment are courses of action that Japanese firms will not be able to ignore in the years to come. Direct investment offers a way to make the best use of accumulated managerial resources and provides the firm with an opportunity to put down roots in international economic society.

---

* One member of the discussion group expressed the opinion that the Japanese government should adopt regulations that would prevent direct investment by Japanese firms from causing an overly competitive situation in the host country. Other members questioned the appropriateness of such regulations, however, and pointed out that they would be very difficult to apply. Some participants in the discussion argued that more detailed measures should be prepared to ensure that direct investment is in harmony with the economy of the host country. Specifically, it was suggested that care should be taken to respect the ethical system of the host country and to avoid disturbing indigenous family and social networks. It was also suggested that concerted efforts to train local workers in management and production technologies, without becoming overly concerned with workers' changing jobs, would be vital in encouraging independent development.

Given the significance of direct investment and its importance to Japan, the private-level initiatives discussed above should be supplemented by an active stance on the part of the Japanese government. The government should also provide leadership in formulating policies that require international consensus.

Such necessary policies include, first, scrupulous planning to ensure an efficient transfer of skills and technologies. In addition to corporate efforts, public measures free from the constraints of the profit motive should also play a part. These measures, which are discussed in detail in a following section, include encouraging international exchange in research and development; promoting the exchange of researchers and students; and expanding educational and training opportunities for engineers from abroad. In considering such measures, we must not forget how greatly Japan's rapid growth in the postwar period benefited from the transfer of technology from Western firms and universities.

Second, particularly in developing countries, there is the risk that an investing firm may find itself embroiled in local conflicts and domestic political disturbances, or have its enterprise nationalized and its management expelled. If firms must face this risk unsupported, they are likely to concentrate their investments in the developed countries, where the risk is lower. But this would mean that Japanese investment avoids the very countries where technology, skills, and knowledge can be utilized most easily. In view of this, policies to reduce country risk must be considered so that more direct investment in the LDCs can take place. For example, such measures as tax incentives and low-interest financing are necessary. In addition, a large-scale, national system of investment insurance should be adopted.

Third, a set of rules based on internationally recognized values will be needed to resolve disputes arising from direct foreign investment. In developed countries, local content requirements and unitary tax laws have recently caused problems, while investments in developing countries face the risk of expropriation and the problems of corporate behavior in the markets of the host country. At present, efforts to devise policies to cope with these problems are primarily made at the bilateral level. In many cases, however, multilateral agreements may result in smoother resolutions.

In concrete terms, this calls for the creation of a system that maximizes the beneficial economic effects of direct investment for both investing and recipient countries. Consideration should be given to the drawing up of rules that will guarantee the free development of direct investment based on a spirit of reciprocity. The feasibility of a multilateral general agreement on direct investment, a counterpart to GATT in the trading field, is worth investigating. Freedom to invest in a non-discriminatory manner should be made the fundamental principle, and standards should be established that regulate national barriers to direct investment. The spirit of reciprocity, however, suggests that exceptions to uninhibited and non-discriminatory direct investment should be allowed for countries with divergent levels of managerial resources. The same sorts of considerations that apply in international trade to protection for infant industries or to emergencies involving industrial adjustment should apply in direct investment.

When GATT was established following World War II as a set of rules governing world trade, only a handful of countries were actually capable of conducting free trade. Yet the introduction of GATT and its ideals contributed immeasurably to the expansion of international trade and the development of the world economy. The same should hold true for an international system regulating direct investments.

Fourth, to ensure the smooth progress of direct foreign investment, it is necessary to consider the formation of a multinational insurance system to cover the losses and reduce the risks incurred due to war, expropriation of investments, inconvertibility of currencies, and so on. This system will make up for the deficiencies of the current national systems in reducing the risks involved in direct foreign investment.

Japan's active participation in the drawing up of this system of rules and international organization, including assistance in terms of expenses, personnel, and knowledge, would be an extremely desirable contribution to the world. By demonstrating to the world its respect for an established set of rules, Japan can help open a path toward conflict-free direct foreign investment. And by taking an active role in a system of collective global management, Japan may gain the good will of other countries in the world.

(d) Encouraging Direct Investment in Japan

The preceding section has dealt with overseas direct investment by Japanese firms. Increasing the pace of direct investment in Japan, however, is a precondition to the smooth development of direct investment from Japan. By investing in Japan, foreign firms will gain access to high-quality production technology, labor, and other factors of production that are available in Japan. Encouraging greater investment in Japan is a necessity. Greater participation by overseas firms in Japanese society will improve mutual understanding through person-to-person contact, and will assist in the internationalization of Japanese firms as well. Thus, Japan will need to adopt an approach that weighs the trend toward increasing direct investment from Japan against the need to increase the level of direct investment in Japan. A balanced flow of direct investment is needed.

Japanese markets will need to become more open to direct investment from abroad. One can, for example, expect foreign service industries to make inroads into the Japanese market, for in this area the accumulation of management know-how in other countries is ahead of that in Japan. Japan must remove barriers that stand in the way of increased investment in this area. As is already being done in some areas, services gathering and providing information about Japanese markets and the investment climate should be consolidated. In addition, financial assistance to encourage direct investment in Japan should be expanded, and a comprehensive system should be developed that fosters investment by providing financial aid, personal introductions, and so on. Trade and other missions should be encouraged, and grievance procedures promoted.

4. Japanese Corporations and Internationalization: International Convergence of Management and "Diversified Sharing"

Corporations will of course be among the major players in the Japanese economy in the 21st century. As mentioned above, business firms have stood in the vanguard of Japan's internationalization. In light of the vital role Japan will continue to play in the world economy, however, Japanese firms will have to become far more international.

(a) The Changing Landscape of Japanese Firms

Tasks for Japanese Firms

To achieve internationalization, Japanese firms will have to come to grips with a number of tasks. First, as noted in the section on direct investment, firms will have to alter their patterns of overseas activity from over-reliance on exports to a more international model that gives greater weight to direct investment and technology transfer.

Second, in order for Japanese firms to internationalize effectively, a fundamental rearrangement of the managerial system is in order. The continued growth of Japan's firms depends in part on their ability to harmonize with the global economy through such adjustments.

Third, it will be necessary for Japanese firms to increase their links with foreign corporations in the international arena. This should include not only partnerships, sharing of technology and parts, and OEM agreements with firms overseas, but also increased links and transactions with foreign firms in Japan. Specifically, measures should include cooperative research and joint ventures, as well as the procurement of parts from abroad.

The New Environment

Japanese firms will have to confront the task of internationalization in the midst of a changing domestic and international environment. The major changes are likely to be the following.

Changes in the action and thinking of the next generation, the pillar of the coming age, are of first importance. Labor mobility may increase as members of the next generation seek self-realization in contexts wider than a single corporation. They may also demand a distribution of benefits based on individual merits.

Liberalization and internationalization of financial and capital markets constitute a second area of change. The internationalization of the capital structure of Japanese firms implies that their management, too, will be susceptible to the logic of international capital.

The rapid pace of technological innovation heralds a third area of change. As we saw in Part I, the new technical discoveries and new applications for technology being made in high technology, space exploration, materials research, nuclear power, and other fields are significantly altering the course of industrialization.

(b) The Basic Tenets of Internationalization

Japanese firms must find methods of management which can effectively grapple with problems of internationalization. The question is: what management principles will be appropriate for the task?

In formulating such principles, two basic requirements must be met. First, the application of these principles must result in corporate activity that is acceptable to other nations of the world, and that contributes to world development. The second requirement is that these principles must be capable of answering the fundamental dilemma of internationalization—that posed by the "localism" of people and the "international" character of capital and technology. In other words, they must be able to respond to the problem of international distribution that arises because people are not easily moved across national borders, while capital and technology readily transcend such boundaries.

Two basic attitudes seem necessary for the further internationalization of Japanese firms.

International Convergence of Management

First, management institutions must be adjusted to accommodate the changed socioeconomic landscape of the future. For example, it is likely that the seniority-wage system will give way to some sort of merit/incentive system. And lifetime employment will probably be applied less generally, making it easier for laborers to change jobs in search of more fulfilling work. The system of corporate labor unions may also change. Japanese corporate management, too, seems destined to undergo organizational and institutional realignment as open and international capital markets expose it more and more to the logic of international capital.

In short, as the international activity of Japanese firms expands, portions of the Japanese management system will have to draw nearer to and more into harmony with foreign practices. Not only will Japanese management practices draw closer to those of foreign systems, but foreign firms will reshape some of their management practices after the existing Japanese model. The movement in the United States to build more cooperative labor-management relations and to make workers partners in the management of the firm attests to this, as does the growing tendency to give more leeway to small-group activities at the workplace and to institute quality control at the company level. This trend among Japanese and foreign corporations to gather on common ground can be termed the international convergence of management.

The major reason for this convergence is that as Japan's society and economy mature, many of the differences in management that distinguish Japanese firms from those of other advanced countries will fade. Another reason is that the characteristics of Japanese management (discussed below) will change in response to the new forms of industrial society being spawned by the new industrial revolution. As the relative demand of more diversified, distinctive products rises, industries in which workers themselves are the chief means of production—the entities that possess the experience and information needed to respond to the values of the consumer—will gradually increase.

Employee-centered Firms and Diversified Sharing

The second principle that will be important in the internationalization of Japanese firms is preservation and development on the domestic front of the basic tenets that have guided their activity thus far, while at the same time adapting them for use in the international arena.

In the period since World War II, Japan has given rise to a form of corporate society in which firms share a number of basic principles. Of these, the most significant for the process of internationalization are those that have to do with the concept of the firm and with "sharing."

Japanese firms tend to be employee-centered. Employee, as used here, refers especially to long-term, core members of the firm, and includes both workers and their representatives, the managers. (Hereafter, "employee" will be used in this broader sense to signify the firm's core members.)

A look at actual management practices in Japanese firms, therefore, reveals that often employees, not stockholders, are treated as the owners of the firm. Several management philosophies derive from this concept of the firm: priority given to employment stability; emphasis on employee satisfaction, with workers being treated as more than mere sources of labor; administrative teamwork; and stress on developing employees' abilities and skills.

The concept of sharing that characterizes many Japanese firms may be called "diversified sharing." A sharing pattern denotes the way (1) technology (or the opportunity to acquire knowledge about it), (2) the value added to output, and (3) the decision-making authority linking the two are distributed among the capitalists, managers, engineers, workers, and other participants in corporate activities.

Under diversified sharing, the sharing patterns of these three elements are dissimilar. For example, individuals with decision-making authority do not necessarily receive correspondingly high salaries. There is also a strong tendency toward "fairness" or "equalization."

Diversified sharing enables a variety of human desires to be satisfied in a host of ways, and "fairness in sharing" is raised to the level of a principle. This, as a result, strengthens employee motivation and lessens conflicts of interest within the firm. Since no efforts are wasted resolving conflicts over the allotment of shares, it becomes easier to devote one's energies to making the corporate "pie" bigger. The upshot is a setup in which all participants cooperate in growth-oriented corporate activities. This concept of the firm has created a socioeconomic system marked by two unique characteristics. One is that the participants in corporate activity do not view one another as having sharply conflicting interests. The other is that the firm is managed not by a few elite employees, but rather by all the members of the firm. These two characteristics have proved a major driving force for Japan's economic development.

Two points must be noted here. The first is that the universality referred to above is not a function of the specific management systems employed by Japanese firms. It is doubtful that seniority wages, lifetime employment, enterprise unions, and other aspects of the legendary "Japanese management system" are internationally applicable. As mentioned above, a good deal of international convergence will have to take place with regard to specific management practices. What do seem universally valid are the basic principles of the system: the employee-centered concept of the firm and the notion of diversified sharing. As these universal concepts are applied across time and national boundaries, however, they may take on very different institutional shapes.

The other point is that employee-centered firms and diversified sharing are not found only among Japanese firms. Many firms in other countries employ these ideas. Nor do these concepts characterize all Japanese corporations. In Japan, however, such firms are in the mainstream.

(c) Formulating a Response

The application of these two principles in different countries, or even in different groups within the same country, would create an international framework for corporate activity that embraces various peoples and different countries. In other words, they create a mechanism through which, for example, the Japanese and non-Japanese within Japanese firms can cooperate in enlarging the overall pie instead of disputing over its distribution. These principles potentially allow many people from all over the world to share the fruits of corporate activity.

Japanese Corporate Principles in the International Arena

Whether this potential can be realized depends on how well Japanese firms can rearrange the institutions based on these principles for application on a global scale. One key lies in employee-centrism, which calls for the inclusion of core employees of overseas subsidiaries in the parent company. They should enjoy employment stability and be allowed to learn the overall operation through job rotation, participate in decision-making, and be enrolled in skills-training programs. The personnel system of the parent company should be able to accommodate foreigners.

In an international context, "diversified sharing" has two

concrete implications. First, as touched on in the section on direct investment, many people from outside Japan would become participants in the sharing. They would take part not only in the distribution of value-added or technology, but in decision-making and ownership as well. The distribution of the latter among a broader group of colleagues can only benefit Japanese firms in the long run.

Second, the sharing patterns should be tailored to match the particular conditions of different countries. For example, if labor conditions in a certain country render the value-added sharing pattern (that is, wage determination) the key to obtaining skilled personnel (as, for instance, is the case among foreign exchange dealers in New York), then the sharing pattern should be adjusted to give the major share of decision-making authority to Japanese employees and the major share of the value-added to local employees. In another country, technology sharing may be the best way to attract qualified people. By adjusting the sharing patterns for the three variables, a firm can respond effectively to conditions in different countries while upholding the principle of fairness. There is only one variable in unilateral sharing, but diversified sharing, like a multi-variable equation, has many solutions.

Overcoming Obstacles

Standing in the way of internationalization are the difficulties which arise when firms develop across international borders. The fundamental problems fall mainly into two areas. First are difficulties involving interaction with peoples of different languages and cultures. Second are problems incurred in confronting labor and capital markets, and distribution systems that are constructed differently.

The first of these is likely to present severe problems for Japanese firms, as they have had little experience with including foreigners among the core members of the firm. Unless Japanese firms can break through this barrier, they will not be able to truly internationalize. How Japanese firms meet this challenge hinges on their acceptance into the global community, the scale of their contribution to world development, and, in the long run, their own profits.

The second trouble area is language. As the core membership of the firm becomes multicultural, in order for sharing to take place on a global scale, close communication within the firm will be necessary. The problem is, in what language should this communication take place? The use of English as the official international language in intra-firm conferences and communications offers a fundamental way around this problem. More widespread use of Japanese by foreigners is, of course, important, but so, too, is improved English language instruction.

The second set of problems arises from contact with various overseas markets. Capital markets which operate on the principle that ownership of the firm rests with the stockholders and labor markets in which labor mobility is high and wages the key determinant of labor movements may not be conducive to employee-centered firms or to diversified sharing. However, Japanese corporations should be able to carve out an enclave within the foreign market which is sufficiently large for them to implement their principles. They must persevere in such efforts, while explaining their cause in a language and manner that is internationally understood.

(d) The Contribution of Japanese Firms

If Japanese firms can successfully apply these corporate principles to the process of internationalization, they can contribute to world progress. This in itself should make the process easier.

Corporate contributions to the world are usually economic or technological. By providing high-quality products, firms can help to raise living standards. Similarly, firms offer employment opportunities, transfer technology, and develop new technologies. In addition, firms (or the entire corporate society of a nation) can make a contribution that is of world historical significance. Providing the world with principles and ways of thinking for a new corporate system is one example.

It is clear that a nation's corporate system must not be forced on the world. Just as Japan, of its own accord, chose certain aspects of Western civilization, the system must be diffused naturally, with each nation making a rational choice, based on independent judgment. For this sort of diffusion to occur, however, the principles of the new corporate system will need to be explained to the world in a form that allows them to be understood. The characteristics of the Japanese system and the way it works must be explained to the world. Applying the principles of employee-centrism and diversified sharing may enable Japanese firms to be accepted in foreign markets with minimal friction. This is the most desirable outcome.

A New Blend of Activities for Corporations

In the future, Japanese corporations will no longer be able to concentrate exclusively on economic performance. This activity must involve a mixture of non-economic elements. Corporations will cease to be solely economic entities; their performance will be judged not only by its economic efficiency, but also by its cultural refinement, political understanding, and humanity.

Although not directly related to management, it also seems likely that the relationship between Japanese corporations and the Japanese government will change. In view of the growing diversity of corporate activity, a new industrial policy might concern itself with establishing a base from which industries or corporations can independently come to grips with the tasks of internationalization.

Portrait of an Internationalized Leader

The managers who lead the internationalization of Japanese firms must possess two characteristics in particular. Just as corporations will no longer be able to concentrate exclusively on economic performance, managers will need to be broadly conversant with trends in politics, economics, culture, and society. Future business leaders should be independent individuals who can act as private-sector diplomats and opinion leaders in the countries with which they work.

The other characteristic required of the new corporate leaders is that they be more than mere organization men. They must be rational and adventuresome, people filled with the entrepreneurial spirit. The leaders of Japan's internationalization must be willing at times to risk the unknown, and they must take the initiative in adapting the principles of Japanese corporations to the international environment.

5. Human, Scientific, and Technological Exchanges: Japan as a Locus for International Exchange

(a) The Significance of Human Exchange

Material, financial, and human exchange are all part of today's growing global interdependence. Of these, we can say that human exchange is the most difficult to promote. As long as human relations lag behind other forms of international exchange, the countries involved may neither sufficiently recognize the extent to which international interdependence is increasing, nor come to a proper understanding of the societies with which they have ties. If we wait for problems to arise before we address this issue, it may well be too late to avoid misunderstandings and antagonism.

Japan may provide a clear example of this troubling state of affairs. In the process of developing the postwar economy, the Japanese focused far more on the material and financial forms of international exchange than on the human. This has surely proved to be a stumbling block to Japan's international relations, exacerbating frictions and confrontations with other nations.

If, along with a recognition of interdependence, there is progress in international human exchange, countries which maintain direct relations will come to appreciate each other's points of view. People all over the world, despite their different lifestyles and cultures, must recognize their interdependence and attempt to better understand one another. This mutual understanding will enable one people to see things from the perspective of another people, giving rise to a sense of solidarity which will, in turn, strengthen political and economic relations. Japan's role should be to promote international communication which can correct the imbalance between material and financial exchange and human exchange. In addition, Japan should contribute to international society by facilitating the sort of worldwide human exchange that will foster global community consciousness.

We can classify international human exchange in several ways. One way is in terms of time. Participation in conferences or meetings abroad is a relatively short-term form of human exchange, while overseas study and business activities involve longer time periods. Immigration—transferring the base of one's life—obviously belongs to the long-term category. Alternatively, we can classify human exchange in terms of how readily the form it takes can be understood by people from different cultures. For example, music, sports, and fine arts are of general interest to people all over the world, while academic and business activities are specialized and demand considerable effort by those who seek to understand or participate in them. Human exchange that demands the transformation of every aspect of human life, such as immigration to an unfamiliar country where one must adjust to an "inscrutable" culture and lifestyle, clearly belongs to the most difficult type in this classification system.

The type of international exchange that we are most concerned with here, and most want to promote, is the academic and business variety, in which Japan is most out of step with the times. Because such human exchange involves a relatively long-term stay abroad and requires considerable cultural adjustment, its promotion requires great efforts. However, this form of exchange has a strong impact on both the host country and the participant's native land.

(b) Exchange at the Level of Daily Life

The Japanese approach to human exchange has tended to be one-sided, with Japanese students and researchers dispatched to the advanced nations to bring back knowledge and technology to Japan. This one-way traffic cannot really be considered "exchange" at all. What is needed from now on is true exchange. Japan should invite talented people from both advanced and developing nations, as well as sending Japanese all over the world. Through this process, Japan can help to advance the worldwide transfer of knowledge and technology. Particularly worth emphasizing here is the fact that the people who come to Japan will come to understand the lifestyle and values of the Japanese people as they really are.

International human exchange does not necessarily result in immediate harmony. Frictions and misunderstandings often occur. As opportunities for exchange increase, however, needless misunderstanding can be prevented if each nation makes an effort to explain its own culture to its partners.

Of course, various aspects of Japanese culture have already been introduced to the world. This cultural interchange, though, has centered on the fine arts, such as music and painting, or on traditional forms of entertainment like Noh, Kabuki, and the tea ceremony—areas of Japanese culture which appeal directly to human feelings. They are readily appreciated, without need for explanation, by people of other nations.

However, it is no longer enough to exhibit only these specific aspects of Japanese culture to the world. To promote an understanding based on an awareness of the lifestyle and values of the Japanese, it is important that people from other countries be able to have direct contact with Japanese people in daily life. Thus, opportunities should be provided for this kind of contact to take place, which will give more and more foreigners a chance to learn about the economic activities and daily concerns of the Japanese people. These experiences will constitute a new form of exchange, centering on culture as it is reflected in daily life.*

To make the experience of living in Japan more fruitful, there should be more opportunities for foreigners to learn about daily life in Japan, through study of the Japanese language and the way of thinking related to it, and of Japanese thought and social structure. Overseas facilities and teaching materials for instruction in the Japanese language and Japanese society should be expanded and improved. In particular, since the number of people desiring to learn Japanese has soared in recent years, the number of overseas language centers has to be increased accordingly. Second, it is necessary to facilitate the stay of foreigners in Japan by expanding Japanese language training and public counseling facilities. Volunteer efforts from Japanese should be encouraged in such community projects. Third, more foreign children should be accepted into the Japanese educational system.

(c) Japan's Role in International Research Exchange

The international circulation of scientific and technological knowledge was greatly facilitated by postwar developments in the

---

* In this regard, one member suggested that more effort should go into creating opportunities for exchange outside the large cities like Tokyo.

fields of communication and education which took place within the stable world economic system. As a small country trying to catch up with Europe and the United States, Japan imported science and technology in massive doses. By improving and adapting this imported technology, Japan was able to lay a foundation for constructing competitive industries, which, in turn, helped it attain rapid economic growth.

We must not forget that in the process of achieving these economic advances, Japanese students and researchers were invited to participate in the highest-level research activities in Europe and the U.S. These Japanese, who absorbed knowledge and carried it back to Japan, were immensely important in the creation of Japan's high level of science and technology. Now that Japan's economy is highly developed, and now that much science and technology in Japan compares favorably with that in Europe and the U.S., it is time for Japan to move beyond the role it has played up until now—that of merely receiving—to that of actively disseminating science and technology throughout the world. By developing and expanding research activities, Japan should seek to open up new frontiers in technology and industry, thereby becoming a leading center for the international exchange of research. Most important, Japan should strive not only to cultivate the technology of the future but also to share the results of its research with the nations of the world.

In asking how Japan can contribute to the world in terms of science and technology, we first need to consider what characterizes "Japanese" science and technology. First, the vast majority of those who carry out research in Japan, both at universities and at research institutes, are Japanese. If a researcher from overseas joins them, the results of his or her research are generally seen as belonging to his or her native country. As a result, research in Japan tends to be rather inbred. In many of the world's leading research centers, an entirely different tendency prevails. For example, since the end of World War II, top-notch researchers from all over the world have gathered in the U.S., where their collective studies have given rise to all kinds of innovations and epoch-making inventions. If Japan is to make a meaningful contribution, all research carried out in Japan, by both Japanese nationals and others, should be geared to developing science and technology which will serve the entire world. Japan should seek to become a locus for international research exchange, and should also oversee the dispersal of the fruits of this research to the other nations of the world.

Basic research is the driving force behind new developments in science and technology, and if Japan is to become a center of worldwide research exchange, efforts must be made to promote basic research, which has lagged behind applied research in Japan. There are, however, many hurdles to be overcome in this regard. Basic research is enormously costly; its results are unknown, and its outcome is seldom directly linked with the needs of industry. In addition, the results of basic research can hardly be kept secret or monopolized for private ends, but tend instead to spill over into the public domain, becoming a sort of public property. However, it is precisely because of this semi-public character that basic research, if it becomes a sort of international public property, can be a crucial ingredient in creating a worldwide collective management system.

It is very difficult to connect basic research with research on applied technology, especially at the level of actual development and production. The outcome of basic research conducted at universities and public research institutes is particularly hard to utilize in developing technologies for private enterprise. Private corporations are reluctant to use basic research in its embryonic stage because it is virtually impossible to ascertain the potential for profitability. One way of closing the gap between basic and applied research might be to link the various academic, governmental, and industrial interests involved in the process of basic research through a research development system. A system of this kind, by facilitating relevant interchange at the human level, would make for a closer connection between basic and applied research.

Japan has historically given priority to applied research—as is illustrated by the fact that the University of Tokyo's Faculty of Engineering is the oldest university engineering department in the world—and thus has a responsibility to assist in advancing applied research throughout the world. To make proper use of the results of basic research, applied research must survey the special characteristics of consumer demand in the marketplace, and formulate new industries and technologies from the results of basic research. This process involves its own type of creativity, which will be important in developing new forms of technology to meet the needs of various countries around the world.

The dimension of human exchange—in particular, the exchange of researchers and technologists—must be a part of both the development of these new technologies and their spread throughout the world. If Japan succeeds in promoting this much-needed human exchange, it can then play a part in the worldwide development of industry while reducing the threat of protectionist measures against high-technology industries. That such protectionism is already on the rise only underscores the importance of promoting both kinds of research and the human exchange on which they depend.

(d)   Accelerating Exchange at Various Levels

To summarize, as part of its expanded role as a member of the global community, Japan should strive to promote worldwide human, scientific, and technological exchange. Exchange at various levels—the exchange of students, educators, researchers, technologists, and businessmen—will go a long way toward creating a sense of mutual international understanding.

Welcoming Students from Abroad

Although more and more foreign students are coming to Japan every year, their number can scarcely be compared with the number of Japanese students overseas. In order to attract capable foreign students, allowing them to participate in different fields within Japanese society, and eventually encouraging them to contribute to progress in their native lands, we need at least to revise the following five aspects of the education of foreign students in Japan.

First, in order to attract college students to Japan, an internationally acclaimed university education and a system designed to admit and accommodate foreign students are needed. No matter how many preparations for hosting foreign students are made, if the international appraisal of the level of education is low, such efforts will surely be undermined. It is a fact that Japanese university degrees, as well as the educational experiences of foreign students in Japan, are not highly esteemed abroad. One result is that many foreign students lose the motivation to study. In any case, it is apparent that many foreign students studying in Japan are dissatisfied and disappointed with the quality of education at Japanese universities.

Second, Japan should provide people from other countries with more opportunities to study at Japanese universities and to obtain employment in Japan. Because of limited openings at Japanese universities, foreign students cannot be certain of being able to study at the university of their choice, even if they have received scholarships from the Japanese government. This is probably one major component in their dissatisfaction with the Japanese educational system. In addition, opportunities for employment after graduating from a Japanese university are extremely limited. This situation is a far cry from the treatment received by Japanese students in foreign countries, such as the United States.

Third, Japan should revise the academic calendar. At present students can begin study only in April. Students should have the option of entering or returning to school (or graduating) at least twice a year, for example in April or September. Not only would such a change enable more foreign students to study in Japan; more Japanese students would also be able to study abroad.

Fourth, we need to establish and strengthen counseling programs for foreign students. The image of Japan held by foreign students is, on the whole, not good. One source of this negative image is the tendency for government officials and university authorities to ignore the individual circumstances of foreign students, or to be inflexible in response to their needs. Furthermore, astonishingly few Japanese can give clear answers to questions from foreign students who would like to understand Japan better. At the very least, we can surely provide each university with counselors who can give appropriate advice to foreign students.

Last, we must expand the system by which students are accepted from abroad. Since the end of World War II, about 5,000 Japanese have studied in the U.S. under the auspices of the Fulbright Program. Japanese who have developed personal ties with

America—and with Americans—by virtue of this program today play major roles in government, business, and academia. To increase the number of foreign students who come to Japan in the future, a major study/human exchange program to bring people to Japan for study needs to be established.* Students should be allowed more freedom and given counsel in their choice of universities and courses. Such a program would be even more effective if it incorporated a way to find foreign students work in, for example, a Japanese company for a certain period after graduation. Working at Japanese firms would enable foreign students to cultivate personal ties with Japanese that would be influential long after they returned to their home countries. Companies could be encouraged to participate in such a program through such measures as tax incentives.

Exchange of Researchers

In order to make Japan a center for the international exchange of research findings, more foreigners should be appointed to teach and carry out research at Japanese universities. This would serve to stimulate further research by their Japanese co-workers and to enliven research activities at Japanese universities. The foreign researchers invited to Japan in the past tended to be world-renowned, established scholars who conducted only short-term

---

* Outline of a Study/Human Exchange Program

Purpose: To strengthen training programs in Japanese language (especially long-term studies for over one year), Japanese society, culture, management, and industrial technology for students, businessmen, engineers and researchers from abroad. At the same time, Japanese language training outside of Japan will be promoted.

Implementation: The following activities will be carried out in connection with the establishment of language training organizations outside Japan (cf. "Exchange at the Level of Daily Life") and the International University of Industry and Culture, as well as existing research and educational institutions.

—well-endowed scholarships and foundations funding studies and research in Japan;

—counseling regarding studies and research in Japan and placement assistance after graduation;

—assistance to Japanese educational and research institutions for the development of curriculum and teaching materials;

—assistance, firstly in the form of sending experts, to overseas institutes involved in the teaching of Japanese language and other subjects related to Japan.

projects. We need to invite more young researchers to carry out longer-term research. In particular, special attention should be given to young scholars from developing countries, many of whom will become the leading researchers in their home countries. Not only will they be able to make good use of the results of work carried out in Japan, but their personal ties with Japan will have a positive influence on future international exchange.

Japan should actively promote international cooperation in governmental R & D projects as well as open its research institutes, such as Tsukuba, to researchers from all over the world. Only in this way can Japan correct the prevailing one-way relationship whereby Japanese researchers go abroad to learn from various nations. The postwar United States was able to attain high levels of development in science and technology, as well as to share the fruits of it with the world, due to its practice of accepting talented researchers from both the advanced nations and developing countries. If Japan aspires to be a center for the exchange of science and technology, it is crucial that it welcome researchers and technologists from all over the world, without regard to nationality or race.

Few researchers at Japanese universities are pursuing area studies in the developing world. Programs should be established immediately to dispatch Japanese researchers to live and carry out research in the developing countries. As well, researchers should be sent to guide their counterparts in the developing nations, and to share with them not only the results of area studies concerning their own parts of the world but also recent developments in science and technology.

Training of Technologists

As we noted in connection with direct investment, the dissemination of technology and skills is best conducted on a person-to-person basis. It is thus essential for Japanese enterprises operating overseas to send technologists to the host country, so that they can work together with that country's technologists in the effective operation of overseas subsidiaries. These firms should also develop programs through which technologists from developing nations can be trained and educated in Japan.

For well over a century, Japanese mid-level technologists have learned foreign technology and applied it to the development of Japanese industry. This was made possible by a high literacy rate resulting from the advanced educational system inaugurated in the Meiji period (1868–1912). In contrast, most of the countries of today's Southeast Asia have low rates of literacy, resulting in a shortage of mid-level technologists. This is certainly one reason why modern technology takes root in Southeast Asian countries only with difficulty, even if other nations try to accelerate the transfer of technology through cooperative measures or direct investment. To help rectify this, Japan must accept people from the developing countries for training. Some of these technologists, upon completing their training, should be allowed to work in Japan. As private enterprises alone cannot provide sufficient training, the Japanese government should take the lead by, for example, improving educational training facilities.

By working for a while in Japan, these foreign technologists will be able to acquire needed skills and also to become familiar with Japan's domestic market. As the number of such technologists grows, they will surely come to play an important role in strengthening the economic ties between their nations and Japan.

(e)   Toward Deepening Mutual Exchange

Work Force Exchanges

Every nation has its own system regulating the entry and departure of foreign nationals. In countries where international exchange includes the acceptance of workers from abroad, there are systems and laws concerning these foreign workers. As part of the global community of the 21st century, Japan needs to examine and revise the rationale and operation of its regulations concerning this type of human exchange. Concerning the entry of foreign workers into Japan, in particular, a reevaluation of present practices cannot be avoided.

The time will come when Japanese and foreigners work together in Japanese offices and factories, and Japanese companies will freely employ qualified foreigners. Such a situation would not only lead to improvements in the Japanese economy, but also have a positive impact on the creation of a global community consciousness. If they were able to get work in Japan more easily, more foreigners would surely choose to study Japanese. Foreign students who were allowed to work as well as study in Japan would return to their home countries with a better understanding of Japan, and could be expected to encourage more of the same kind of human exchange.

One promising sign of the transformation in Japanese attitudes relating to foreign workers is the "Working Holiday" program. This program allows young Japanese, Australians, New Zealanders, and Canadians to travel and work in one another's countries with only a tourist visa. The significance of this program is that it gives members of the younger generation, who will have positions of responsibility in the 21st century, opportunities to experience first-hand the lifestyles and cultures of different peoples. If this program were expanded to include more nations it would surely lead to a gradual widening of personal ties among the world's young people.

There are likely to be formidable obstacles to liberalizing the exchange of workers, particularly those regarding the acceptance of workers from abroad. However, Japan should consider moving gradually toward greater openness vis-à-vis foreign workers. Flexible responses to the issue should be drawn up in the spirit of international exchange and cooperation.

Facilitating Global Human Exchange

To contribute to worldwide human exchange as a member of the global community, Japan must not only promote the exchange of individuals, but also participate in international organizations.

Members of international organizations, such as the United Nations and its related organizations or the International Red Cross, work together to accomplish common goals that extend beyond national boundaries. These organizations compose an invaluable base for constructing a global community. Japan can help these multifaceted, governmental and non-governmental international organizations financially, and also by sending talented Japanese to participate in joint research projects, in international academic conferences or in committees of businessmen from around the world. By taking part in and supporting these activities, Japan can live up to its role as an economic and cultural contributor to the global community.

6. Responding to North-South Problems: Assistance for Independent Development and the Relief of Poverty

The relations between the developing countries and the advanced industrial countries—the so-called North-South problem—is an issue with which the world community has failed to come to grips in the postwar era. According to a World Bank report from 1981, developing countries (i.e., the South) amounted to 159 out of 176 countries in the world and accounted for more than 80% of world population. Their total GNP and exports, however, accounted for only 20% and 30%, respectively, of world totals. In contemplating its role in the global community, Japan should actively concern itself with North-South problems, and take the initiative in implementing their solutions.

(a) The Current State of North-South Problems and Proposals for Their Solution

Economic development of the developing countries must finally be based on their own efforts. Developed countries should extend the assistance needed to make this possible. Thus developed countries must open their markets to exports from the developing world, encourage direct investment, and promote economic and technological cooperation. Measures to resolve the debt problem are also needed. Since weaker growth in the industrial nations may also slow the expansion of markets for products from developing countries, a more active approach to, for example, economic and technological cooperation will be needed to provide developing countries a base to establish independent economic growth. The role of direct investment in this process was discussed in a previous section of this report; here we will consider other issues.

Encouraging North-South Trade

Ideally, economic growth for the developing countries can be achieved by increased exports of products in which they hold a comparative advantage. This is why the developing countries continue to strongly advocate a policy of "trade, not aid." The trade solution, however, did not work out, for several practical reasons.

First, as was noted at the beginning of the discussion of our seven-part proposal, free trade has not been the rule for many of the products and in many of the areas in which developing countries hold a comparative advantage. A large number of the products in which developing countries excel are exempted by GATT from free trade rules or protected in developed countries by high tariffs. Examples include agricultural products, processed agricultural products, and textiles. The Generalized System of Preference (GSP), devised to encourage exports from the developing countries, cannot achieve its intended results because of the extensive exemptions. Consequently, despite the apparent advantages afforded developing countries under the current system of international trade, the terms and conditions of trade still favor developed countries. This situation gave rise to charges that GATT was designed to benefit the developed countries, and led, in turn, to the creation of the United Nations Conference on Trade and Development (UNCTAD) and the New International Economic Order (NIEO).

As we have argued, free trade offers enormous benefits to the world community. If developed countries infringe on the principle of free trade in pursuit of their own interests or in an attempt to protect industries that have irreversibly lost their international competitiveness, then a true solution to North-South problems will remain a distant dream.

Economic instability in the developing countries often leads to political instability, which is a far from desirable state of affairs for developed countries as well. Resolution of North-South problems can only be achieved if the rules of trade are re-adjusted so as to reflect the interests of both developing and developed countries.

To this end, we must first improve the export environment for products from developing countries. GATT rules should be re-evaluated from the standpoint of liberalizing markets in developed countries for agricultural and light industrial products. Japan, as one of the principal beneficiaries of the postwar free trade system and as the second largest market in the free world, can take a leading role in this effort by opening its domestic market to imports from the developing countries.

Over the longer run, we should also consider giving UNCTAD an official position in the international economic order in order to enable it to function more effectively.* Japan is now one of the leading centers of production in the world. By shifting earnings gained from production to balanced encouragement of imports, Japan could provide a large market for imports from the developing countries, particularly in agricultural products, processed agricultural goods, and labor-intensive products. The opening of these markets would undoubtedly cause political strife domestically, but if Japan is to demonstrate its willingness to become a full-fledged member of the international community and a full partner in any system of coordinated management, it should be prepared to tackle these problems aggressively.

At the same time, Japan should redouble its efforts to promote domestic industrial adjustment, technological innovation, and product diversification and to accelerate the vertical division of labor among nations. Such efforts assume even greater importance in light of the ongoing division of labor between Japan and ASEAN and the NICs, whose industrial structures have become increasingly sophisticated in recent years.

While it will be vital in relations with these countries to consider the vertical division of labor, smooth progress in the horizontal (intra-industry) division of labor must also be encouraged. By further promoting the intra-industry division of labor in this area (on the basis of economies of scale, etc.), Japan and its trading partners could help lay the groundwork for stable, mutually beneficial interaction and achieve an efficient allocation of resources. This, in turn, would contribute to the expansion of trade and the improvement of economic utility in each nation. Given the importance of close communication and technical cooperation among industries, governments of the participating nations must also take the initiative in promoting this sort of exchange.

---

* One member of the Round Table argued that GATT and UNCTAD should perhaps be combined into a single international economic organization.

Stabilizing the Prices of Primary Products

Another factor behind the sluggish growth of exports from the developing countries is the fragility of their trade structures. The prices of primary products, their chief exports, are very unstable and easily affected by depressed markets and fluctuations in exchange rates. Primary products in general have much less price elasticity of demand than manufactured goods—that is, price changes cause little change in demand. Therefore, changes in export prices, whether caused by market movements or by exchange rate fluctuations, soon show up as trade imbalances, which is exactly what has been happening to the developing countries over the past several years. Economic stagnation in the developed countries has caused commodity prices to plummet. This, coupled with the steady appreciation in value of the U.S. dollar, triggered an economic crisis in many developing countries. The appreciation of the dollar meant, on the one hand, a decrease in the price of dollar-denominated exports and a drop in export revenue calculated on a dollar basis. On the other, it meant that dollar-denominated imports became more expensive. In either case, the trade balance of the exporting country worsened when no adjustment in the quantity of exports occurred.

A number of solutions to the price problem have been attempted in the past, including price maintenance agreements among commodity producers and the creation of inventory adjustment funds for primary products. But even OPEC, the Organization of Petroleum Exporting Countries, by far the most powerful and successful of such schemes, now finds its base considerably weakened by philosophical divisions among its members and by pricing policies that paid no heed to conditions in oil-importing countries. It follows, then, that it will be even more difficult to achieve long-term price stability in mining or agriculture, given the existence of large numbers of outsiders (free-riders) and potential new entrants.

Through the beginning of the 21st century, however, developing countries will by and large remain suppliers of primary goods. Over the coming 20 or 30 years, therefore, stable prices for primary goods will still be essential for the development of these countries. The fundamental solution to this problem is to build a more stable structure of export industries in developing countries through their own efforts and with support from the industrialized nations. When a more stable industrial structure is achieved, developing countries will not need to depend on a single primary good whose price is quite unstable.

An economically viable solution would be one that alleviates the adverse effects arising from short-term swings in commodity prices, while maintaining pricing based on the market mechanism over the long term. To build an international system of this sort would be difficult without the participation of both producers and consumers. The consumers (i.e., the industrialized countries) would benefit from long-term stability in supplies and prices of primary products, and could then share some of the financial burden, in the form, for instance, of an inventory adjustment fund. Participation by the developed countries in such a system would also serve to maintain a quasi-market mechanism while avoiding detachment of commodity pricing from market movements. Also, given the problem of outsiders, such a system should be organized on a multi-product, rather than product-by-product, basis.

Certain experts argue that price maintenance agreements should be discouraged because they interfere with effective re-source sharing. They contend that the growth of developing countries would be better served by economic assistance, adjusted to price fluctuations in primary products. This argument deserves close inspection, but there is the danger that such assistance may lead to competition to increase trade losses in order to gain a greater portion of the aid. Since detailed rules would therefore be needed to create a suitable aid system, such a system would in the end differ only slightly in function from multilateral price maintenance.

In addition, priority ought to be given to the management of exchange rates, in light of both its feasibility and its significance for the North-South problem. As noted above, the flow of capital has recently played a greater role in determining exchange rates than has trade. In the realm of capital flows, however, the develop-ing countries have few effective means of recourse. Their financial markets are underdeveloped, and, unlike developed countries, they can exert little, if any, influence on international exchange rates through manipulation of domestic financial policy. Nor do they have the reserves of foreign currency needed to effectively intervene in currency markets. In this sense, their predicament is far more severe than that of the developed countries, which can respond to currency problems by policy adjustment or coordination.

For the sake of sound economic management in the less developed countries (LDCs), the developed countries should join together in a coordinated effort to create an environment where exchange rates reflect the economic fundamentals of the respective countries. Macro-level policy coordination by the developed countries to achieve exchange rate stability would be economically beneficial both to themselves and to the LDCs, and should therefore be given high priority. Japan, as one of the major economic powers whose strength is likely to persist in the foreseeable future, should take a leading role in this effort.

The Debt Problem

Growing international debt poses serious problems for developing nations, particularly the nations of South and Central America and certain countries in Asia. Developing countries typically have underdeveloped infrastructures, the improvement of which is hampered by a lack of domestic capital. These countries are obliged to borrow the necessary funds from abroad. The accumulation of some debt is therefore unavoidable. Problems arise when the borrower country is no longer able to meet its debt obligations. This situation often occurs when debt rises faster than exports, the usual source of funds for debt repayment. Once caught in this quagmire, a nation will see its fiscal burden escalate and its predicament worsen steadily.

The fundamental resolution of these problems lies in the hands of the developing nations. They must possess a realistic vision of their economic future and shape concrete measures for debt alleviation accordingly. The developed countries, for their part, should give consideration to short-term relief through debt moratoria and the like.

In the long run, the best hope for a solution may lie in enhancing the functioning of the International Monetary Fund and the World Bank, while improving the export environment of the developing countries. In short, the same sorts of measures that were outlined above in respect to primary and light industry imports seem to offer the most desirable solution to the debt problem as well.

Economic and Technical Cooperation

There are two kinds of economic and technical cooperation. The first is assistance that supports or facilitates economic growth in the developing countries and acts to deepen interdependence. The second is cooperation to relieve famine and poverty. The two cannot in actual practice be differentiated so clearly, but for the sake of analysis we will do so here. In this section, the former type of cooperation will be considered; the latter will be treated in the next section.

Overseas Development Assistance (ODA) by and large flattened out in 1980, despite UN General Assembly resolutions in 1970 and again in 1980 which set a target of 0.7% of GNP for ODA from the developed countries. As of 1983, only five nations had met this goal: Norway, the Netherlands, Sweden, France, and Denmark. ODA functions as a redistributive mechanism to relieve the great income disparities among nations, and the target level is by no means too high. In the long run, the ODA target will probably need to be revised again, but for the time being, all possible effort should be devoted to realizing the current 0.7% goal.

Past effort to expand ODA has made Japan the world's second largest provider of ODA, and international acclaim for this achievement is high. However, Japan's ratio of ODA to GNP is far below the 0.7% target level, and somewhat behind the average for DAC (Development Assistance Committee) members. Thus Japan must continue its current effort to increase ODA expenditures. Greater care needs also to be taken in tailoring assistance to meet the actual needs of developing countries. Japanese technical and economic assistance should be designed to encourage economic independence in developing countries. Specifically, Japanese assistance should encourage development of export or import substitution industries, which will help developing countries gain new supplies of foreign currency or preserve existing reserves. Japanese assistance should also focus on preparing industrial infrastructure and on developing small and medium enterprises, which serve as supporting industires. Technical cooperation should also be increased, by sending greater numbers of technical personnel abroad, extending yen loans and grant aid, or other methods. The various tools should be combined organically in order to maximize the beneficial effects of cooperation. As stressed in other parts of this report, technology transfer through direct investment, governmental and industrial research cooperation, and technical cooperation brought about by greater interchange with people from developing countries will also be important. Technologies are transferred efficiently on a person-to-person basis, and the Japanese efforts in this area have been well received.*

(b) Responding to Poverty and Famine

Both the pessimism of Malthus and the Club of Rome's warnings about the "limits of growth" are based on the assumption that the world's supply of resources is finite and therefore population will inevitably increase at a rate higher than the growth rate of marginal productivity. A great many arguments have been advanced both for and against this view, but at present most of the developed and developing countries seem to share an optimistic prognosis about the possibility of growth through technological innovation.

In certain—primarily African—developing countries, however, population growth seems destined to outstrip the growth of production no matter how optimistic one's suppositions about growth and other factors are. Mortality in these countries has dropped steadily since World War II, and the average lifespan has lengthened rapidly. Industrial production in these mainly agricultural countries simply cannot keep pace with the swelling population.

Many factors contributed to this state of affairs, but the most important probably were, first, tardiness in coming to grips with the population problem and, second, faulty agricultural policy. To feed the burgeoning populations, land has been opened with

---

* It was pointed out that projects to attract Japanese tourists and stimulate export to Japan—thereby increasing employment and gaining long-term foreign currency income—should be emphasized, and that Japan should guarantee markets for these projects for a certain period.

little regard for ordering development. This has contributed to a loss of arable land and the advance of desertification, and, as a result, a marked decrease in the fertility of land in some areas. The World Bank and others highlight these policy problems and emphasize the importance of self-help on the parts of the nations involved.

Practically speaking, however, we must realize that policy options are few for the affected countries. Large families are economically expedient in many low-income countries. Children, after they reach the age of 10 or so, are a valuable source of labor, and the more children a family has the greater is its income-earning capacity. Thus birth rates are generally quite high in low-income countries, rendering solutions for the population problem more difficult. The same is true of agricultural policy. For instance, while the removal of all restriction on supply and demand or pricing for daily commodities may encourage producers to produce more, consumers may thus find it impossible to make ends meet. Other means to increase productivity, such as improvements in agricultural technology, also take time.

The response to the plight of these nations must encompass both governmental and private sectors. On the private level, greater recognition of the problem of poverty and famine is needed. In addition, tax measures to provide financial support for voluntary activities by firms should be considered.

Cooperation to develop irrigation and other infrastructure, for afforestation programs, woodland preservation, technical assistance in seed programs and desalinization, etc., should be extended toward countries suffering from desertification and loss of arable land. Poverty and famine are precisely the sort of problems that should be met with an effort by the global community.

The Japanese response to crisis situations caused by natural disasters has often been criticized as inadequate, particularly in terms of human assistance. In famine and disaster relief, human aid is generally superior to economic assistance. While it may be impossible to answer all calls for assistance, Japan should press ahead with plans to develop a flexible system of response to crises in other parts of the world. This system should involve both the government and the private sector.

7. Security and World Peace: Toward Regional Stability

The postwar international system, as noted above, is shifting from one overwhelmingly dominated by the United States, chiefly in the world economy, to a collective management system centered around the United States. However, in the realm of military affairs, the East-West balance of power based on U.S.-Soviet bipolarity continues to prevail. The American dominance in military and security affairs in the West is most likely to continue. Japan's basic approach to military and security affairs, therefore, is to accommodate to changes in the U.S.-Soviet balance, and its role there should be different from its role as a major and active supporter of the collective economic management system.

Any discussion of the stability and growth of a multidimensional international society transcending national boundaries must consider the matter of global security and military affairs, and Japan's approach to these questions is very important. The following is an overview of trends in the international military situation and global security in the remaining years of the 20th century, with a consideration of Japan's role and responsibilities in that context. We will also examine Japan's role in the resolution of regional conflicts, and ways in which it can facilitate growth and stability in an increasingly interdependent international society by cultivating heightened consciousness of the global community.

Japan in the East-West Balance

The confrontation between the United States and the Soviet Union is not limited to the narrow concerns of security. It also involves ideological conflict and diplomatic rivalry. Of the many facets of U.S.-USSR (East-West) relations, the most significant today is the military-security dimension. In view of the overwhelming military superiority of both countries, the Soviet-American bipolar military structure, sustained by nuclear deterrence, will remain basically unchanged through the beginning of the 21st century, although the military balance between

Washington and Moscow may well shift, at least relatively. Politically, there will continue to be cycles of increased tension and relaxed relations. For Japan, the key question is what specific policies it should adopt vis-à-vis the military aspects of the East-West bipolar structure.

In examining Japan's role, let us look at the view that the stability of the East-West balance attained by U.S.-Soviet nuclear deterrence is a kind of international public good. Expansion of one country's military expenditures may lead to instability, particularly in neighboring countries. Basically, therefore, military expenditures cannot be called the shouldering of a share in providing international public goods. However, in the sense that nuclear deterrence guarantees the security not only of the United States but of other Western countries against the political and military power of the Eastern bloc nations centering on the Soviet Union, it is possible to consider such deterrence a kind of international public good for the Western bloc in the realm of security.

Since the end of World War II, the United States has provided the public international goods for Western security. It will continue to do so, but maintaining stability in the bipolar East-West system depends largely on the future course of development of the two superpowers' economic strength and technology. The United States, for example, is both the economic and military leader of the West, and maintaining the position requires enormous public expenditures for military and other purposes. This may be a major reason for the huge fiscal deficit now besetting the United States. (The Stockholm International Peace Institute gives these figures on shares of world military expenditures for 1984: United States 31%, NATO total 50%, Soviet Union 22%, WTO total 24%.)

Japan must be fully aware of the cost shouldered by the United States for these international public goods. As a major supporter of the collective management of the world economy, Japan ought to bear a burden of international public goods commensurate with its economic strength. Given the importance to Japan of the U.S.-Japan security system, and also given Japan's role as a member of the Western camp, it should also consider its share of the cost of defense.

One of Japan's basic policies is that it will not directly intervene militarily in any armed conflict. This fundamental stance is unlikely to change in the years leading up to the turn of the century. Japan must continue to maintain its defense-oriented posture, improving the quality of its defense capability in line with the U.S.-Soviet balance and the regional situation.

It is important that Japan firmly refrain from activities that might increase international tension, such as a military build-up. It can help to stabilize international politics and contribute to stable development of the North-South relationship through economic and technical cooperation and assistance, and other indirect methods.

From an intermediate and long-range perspective, Japan can work to improve U.S.-Soviet relations through efforts for nuclear non-proliferation, arms control, and arms reduction. It is also necessary for Japan to make patient and steady efforts to turn the United States and the Soviet Union away from a relationship heavily oriented to military concerns and toward more constructive economic ties. A strong military is not the only way in which a country can contribute to its own and the world's security. A stable economy, for example, is the essential element of security for a given nation or the region of which it is a part. Japan should give priority to policies that will help stabilize the regional and global economy, thereby contributing in an ancillary fashion to international security.

Although Japan's role will be chiefly economic, it must take a more active role in international politics in accordance with its economic strength and give greater consideration than in the past to global security.

Japan's Contribution to Regional Stability

The United States and the Soviet Union will continue to exert considerable influence in regional conflicts, but the mechanism of East-West stability through nuclear deterrence will have little direct effect on the resolution or prevention of regional hostilities. The important point here is that regional economic stability will promote social and political stability and work, in turn, to prevent disputes from escalating to the level of armed conflict. This demonstrates the importance for Japan, in its treatment of regional disputes, of promoting economic and thus—indirectly—political stability, based on the conditions of interdependence in the international economy.

There are networks of military deterrence and balance at work in the Asian region—between the United States and the Soviet Union, between China and Vietnam, between the ASEAN countries and Indochina, between South and North Korea, and between the Soviet Union and China—yet the military balance is delicate and fluid. In this network, the United States has established itself as the leading force for maintaining the security of the region as a whole. The Soviet Union is likely to be more concerned with cultivating its own position and interests in Asian affairs, and it is fully predictable that, while it may not be able to increase its military presence there, it may eventually establish diplomatic and political footholds in the region. China will continue its amiable, cooperative ties with Japan and the United States and play an important role in the future of the Asian region through its relations with those nations and with Indochina, the Korean peninsula, and the Soviet Union.

Relations between the great powers, as determined by the Soviet and U.S. military presence in the Far East, by China's foreign policy, and by other factors, will greatly affect future stability in Asia. It is extremely important that Japan be fully congnizant of the need for balance in the regional situation in considering the share of the cost of international public goods, including security; economic interdependence with the Soviet Union; and economic cooperation with China.

As regimes in various Asian countries change in the later years of the current decade and in the 1990s, there is a likelihood that internal politics will destabilize over issues involving political systems and succession, as the recent turmoil in the Philippines demonstrates. Abrupt economic or social changes may cause greater inequities and further social stratification, and these developments can, in turn, provoke the rise of extremist forces and further destabilize the socioeconomic order. Such movements tend to be strongly nationalistic and anti-foreign, and they have an impact on international cooperation and regional peace.

Uncertainty and dissatisfaction have been increasing among the new middle classes in many Asian countries over the past several years. If the present rates of rapid growth do not continue, dissatisfaction with current administrations and the established order may grow. Domestic instability in particular countries will probably pose the greatest threat to international and regional stability in the next 10 to 20 years. In the Asian region, basically it is economic instability that may lead to social and political instability, and thence to military conflict.

It is important for Japan, which has a vital stake in the stability and prosperity of Asia, to pay close attention to the regional situation, including localized disputes, and to the military balance among the United States, the Soviet Union, China, and other powers, and work to prevent conflicts before they break out. It must give priority to regional economic cooperation and interdependence, extending economic and technological assistance and working to construct a stable North-South economic order that will enhance regional political stability. As an example of regional economic cooperation, ASEAN's achievements are particularly noteworthy. ASEAN is not an organization intended to rally military resistance to powers from outside the region, but one that concentrates chiefly on fostering economic cooperation and regional unity, and this has worked to reduce armed conflict and antagonism within the region.

More attention should be given to preventing and promoting solutions for armed conflicts on a regional level, as well as at the level of U.S.-Soviet nuclear confrontation. Such conflicts pose an enormous threat to the interdependent relations of international society on which the livelihood of the Japanese people depends. It is necessary for Japan to work as a neutral intermediary, through diplomatic and other channels, for conflict resolution and avoidance of confrontations.

Efforts for Peace through International Organizations

Japan must reaffirm the positive functions of the United Nations and work to solve conflicts, global or regional, through international organizations. Opinion is divided today over the effectiveness of the United Nations, but in the long run it is necessary for Japan to work constructively for sound management of the world body and strengthening of its functions. Japan should not simply pay a large share of UN operating expenses, but also should send capable people to serve in its Secretariat and affiliated agencies.

In the resolution of international disputes, the limits of influence of a third party are well known, but Japan should participate more actively in the peace-keeping activities of international organizations. Japanese should also seriously reflect on the reasons for and the meaning of their country's active involvement in the solution of international disputes, even when its national interest is not directly at stake.

International Conflict Resolution and Global Community Consciousness

Arms control talks between the United States and the Soviet Union and improving the international security system for resolving conflicts or easing tensions are of extreme importance to international society. Still, as noted earlier, contemporary international society is not sustained or controlled by military-security factors alone.

International exchange is now expanding on all levels—in goods and materials, in money, and on the person-to-person level—and this has enhanced the interdependence of all nations. Mutual dependence among countries is growing in the economic, cultural, and social realms, as well as between the North and South and between East and West. As already mentioned, such a trend is inevitably accompanied by a wide variety of frictions on the government, corporate, and individual levels.

Under the stable international system that has prevailed since World War II, there has been rapid and multifaceted increase in the interdependence of all Western nations. Various frictions have arisen as a result, but generally solutions were found within the system because any resort to force of arms in the solution of disputes would have been contrary to the common interest. Increased stability in interdependent relations allows governments, corporations, and people to reach beyond national boundaries to establish multidimensional, multilevel networks. Interdependence tends to undermine conflict between nations, and reduces the effectiveness of military means in conflict resolution.

But because an alternative system has yet to be developed in which all members of international society work together to solve common problems, the nation-state remains the unit for resolving frictions and conflicts arising from increasing interdependence as well as problems that transcend national borders. The possibility always exists that when domestic interests are involved, trade and economic frictions may escalate to the level of international disputes. This could lead to government-initiated economic sanctions and other forms of retaliation, which could destroy even the most deeply entrenched cooperative relationship. When a situation reaches that extreme, the economic rationality of interdependent exchange from which all sides benefit has already been forfeited, and the behavior of a state will be determined by nationalistic values which are the antithesis of global community consciousness.

That is why a system of collective management in which leading countries work together in harmony and solidarity is so important. In such a system nations can construct a stable international economic order that takes disparities into consideration and encourages exchange across national boundaries. Stable interdependent relations built through such a system will also embrace the developing nations. It is a system of crucial importance in preventing international disputes from reaching critical proportions.

Toward Peaceful Conflict Resolution

The East-West bipolar structure, although stabilized through nuclear deterrence, is governed by political-military power and confrontation between nations or blocs of nations—the very antithesis of the idea of global community. The global community as envisaged here, however, is not aimed at establishing a system that can prevent international disputes or conflicts without fail. Confrontation in ideology and values will exist as long as the peoples of the earth cling to their customary ways of thinking. What is most needed today, at the governmental level, is efforts to create a system in which all nations can benefit through interdependence without recourse to arms, and a common awareness and set of values that opposes the resort to armed conflict. At the popular level, a consensus is needed on the importance of peaceful co-existence. In order to cope with interdependence effectively, we must cultivate global community consciousness and improve systems for international exchange that will reflect that consciousness. Each nation-state should coordinate its internal and external interests, and join other states in the task of collective management of international inequities and interchanges and of shaping the international order.

Keeping its position in the West in mind, Japan must clarify the nature of its interdependent relations with the rest of the world, including the nations of the Eastern bloc. The United States and the Soviet Union stand in fundamental confrontation not only militarily and politically but in terms of their basic worldview, and this situation can be expected to continue. But the increasing interdependence of the West is slowly, but steadily, permeating into the East. Establishing such interdependence may not be the most direct way to peace, but closer contact with the Soviet bloc will bring heterogeneous elements into a web of relationships where basic cooperation is the common interest of the nations concerned. Such an eventuality would not only work to Japan's benefit but would help to stabilize and nurture the international community as a whole. Deepened interdependence will not, of course, change the East-West bipolar structure overnight, governed as that structure is by *realpolitik* and military power; nor will it directly affect the political-military structure of the East.

Cooperation in the economic progress of the developing countries through assistance, trade, and investment, and the emergence of stable and interdependent North-South relations, will greatly affect East-West relations, since it will, in effect, bring the Third World into the network of Western interdependence. It is important that interdependence be facilitated in economic, cultural, social, and other areas, and be spread throughout the world. Accumulated efforts in this direction will foster global community consciousness among the peoples of the world.

PART III

Japanese in a Global Community: Internal Internationalization

In Part II, we discussed how "Japan in a global community" can fulfill its proper role and contribute to the world as it enters the 21st century, since its economic position will surely grow increasingly significant.

It is actual people who will have to accomplish these goals. Therefore, whether or not Japan will succeed depends on whether the Japanese people can rise to the task and see to it that the country fulfills its role and makes its contribution adequately.

As mentioned in Part I, the wave of technological innovation is bringing about major changes in industrial society. In addition, Japan's interdependence with the rest of the world is deepening. Against such a backdrop, the Japanese people, particularly the emerging generation, will have ample opportunities to become more in tune with the times. The problem lies in the speed at which this can be accomplished. We hope that if the obstacles that stand in the way of this process and the possible excuses for backsliding can be removed, the lifestyle natural to Japanese will become one that befits the role and contribution of "Japan in a global community."

A. Japanese in an Affluent Society

If stable economic growth continues into the 21st century, Japan's GNP will grow larger, and its level of personal income will also undoubtedly rise to among the world's highest. Japan's GNP, which in 1960 amounted to a mere 4% of the world's GNP, climbed to over 12.4% of the total in 1984.

But can we say that this represents balanced growth? Is there any correlation between the "affluence" indicated by the GNP figures and the "affluence" experienced by the Japanese people?

Consider, for instance, a day in the life of a typical city dweller in Japan. He leaves his cramped quarters every morning, is jostled about during a long commute on a crowded train, reports for duty in an attractive new office building, and works on until late at night. The above description testifies to the disproportion between "flow" side affluence, as reflected in the GNP level, and the "stock" side poverty found in actual Japanese life.

Of course, continued affluence in the "flow" sphere is certain to lead, in due course, to affluence in the "stock" sphere as well. Until then, people in the other advanced nations may regard the Japanese as a people with whom they do not share a common set of values. Japan must act quickly to redress this disproportion between "flow" side affluence and "stock" side poverty.

In this regard, Japan should embark on a program of balanced land development and urban planning to end the over-concentration of resources in Tokyo.

As mentioned in Part II, if Japan is to go forward as a full-fledged member of a global community, to fulfill its role and make its proper contribution, each individual Japanese will be required to assume a share of the burden on a variety of fronts. Japan must not view the "global community" as a society of nations which it can enter at minimal cost while reaping maximum profit. Rather, the global community should be viewed as the most desirable form of international society possible, in which Japanese and the rest of humanity share common values. An international society of this sort entails an enormous commitment on the part of each and every member; should Japan, for example, succumb to short-term interests and attempt to "go it alone" or take a "free ride," it could be considered responsible for having brought about the collapse of the whole system.

But what about the idea that Japanese have an unbalanced image of their own lives—that they do not have any real sense of their affluence? If this is the case, there is the distinct possibility that they will fail to identify with their new international role and the need to make a contribution, and that all that remains will be dissatisfaction with the weight of the burden these impose. People with such a perspective would hardly be supportive of an increased role for Japan in the global community. For this reason, it is necessary for Japanese to stop regarding themselves as deprived and to learn to enjoy an affluence appropriate to their economic strength. The increase in consumption, in investment, and in imports this change would engender could help to correct Japan's trade imbalance and, over the long term, become a new driving force for Japanese growth.

However, this does not imply that failure on the part of the Japanese to reap the benefits of "affluence" would absolve Japan from making an appropriate contribution to the world. The question is, will Japan contribute to the world because it is convinced of the necessity of doing so, or in order to stem the barrage of foreign criticism?

"Affluence" is of course a subjective notion which changes considerably depending on the yardstick one uses to measure it. The standard of "affluence" in Japan will change in accordance with what sort of lifestyles Japanese people are capable of imagining for themselves. If we measure prosperity by the yardstick of society as it will be in the 21st century—i.e., post-industrial society—Japan's current level of affluence seems still quite low, even though all the essential requirements for daily life have been met. For instance, although the average salaried worker may at present be satisfied with his housing, few homes today have enough space for, say, a study room. If study rooms become one of the measures of a leisurely lifestyle, then it follows that a home without one will become a symbol of deprivation. Similarly, the forest of telephone poles and webs of telephone wires that mar the skylines of Japan's cities may soon signify lack of affluence, however efficient they may be. In other words, as standards rise, people may come to expect more than mere functionality.

Viewed in this way, as Japanese face the 21st century and attempt to bring about a society based on a truly balanced affluence, the first requirement is that they give full play to their imaginative powers with regard to lifestyle. To pave the way for a new lifestyle, salaries and leisure time must increase to proper levels. In addition, the government must promote policies aiming at more effective land use and improvement in the living environment —particularly the housing situation—of its people.

To this end, a balanced tax system must be adopted which would allow Japanese to shoulder both the international responsibilities stemming from quantitative affluence and their obligation to bring about qualitative affluence at home.

B. Acceptance of Diverse Value Systems

In the 21st century, Japanese will be active in the global community, and the number of foreigners living in Japan will probably increase dramatically. As human exchanges go forward, and particularly as Japan accepts larger numbers of foreign residents, opportunities for making contact with other cultures will expand. In asking others to understand Japanese lifestyles and values, Japanese must also recognize those of others and strive continuously to ensure harmonious co-existence.

Will Japanese be able to display the level of tolerance such a situation will require? One optimistic view has it that, since Japanese have for hundreds of years been able to harmonize their own various beliefs and world views, they are clearly capable of such tolerance. As stated at the outset of this section, the upcoming generation will have had ample opportunity from youth onward for contact with other cultures and worlds different from their own. Some believe that if the new generation emerges with a different perspective from that of older Japanese, there will naturally be more tolerance of other value systems.

On the other hand, there is a more pessimistic view which has it that the development of a diverse system of values requires a clash of opposing absolutist values. Since Japan has never experienced serious internal religious or social conflict, this view holds that it will be extremely difficult to cultivate a real tolerance for diversity of values. Whichever view is closer to reality, however, Japan can no longer avoid acting as part of the global community. No matter what the hurdles to overcome may be, Japanese must learn tolerance for different value systems and coexistence with people of different lifestyles.

A closely related issue is whether Japan can recognize and accept the growing diversity and heterogeneous elements in its own society. A striking example of the ill effects of standardization and anti-individualism in postwar education is the plight of Japanese children who, having been educated abroad for some years, are labeled "returnees" and often have difficulties gaining acceptance back into the mainstream educational system when their families return to Japan. Similarly, employment opportunities in Japan for graduates from foreign universities is relatively limited.

The way of thinking of Japan's young people is beginning to change. There is now more emphasis on spiritual satisfaction rather than material prosperity, on leisure time and family rather than work and the workplace, and on living for today rather than tomorrow. Therefore, as the first step toward increasing its tolerance for diverse foreign values, Japan should become more accepting of the growing diversity of values in its own midst. Japanese should realize the importance of tolerating diversity in the education system and elsewhere.

C. Japanese with a True Sense of the Global Community

As mentioned in Part I of this report, all human beings are slowly but surely coming to the realization of their interdependence. Growing economic interdependence and common national problems are giving rise to a general recognition of the finiteness of the globe's natural resources as well as to a shared fear of nuclear war.

Having few natural resources and hence forced to rely on imports, Japanese have had vivid, direct experience of the peril of limited resources, most dramatically especially during the oil crisis of 1973. In addition, partly due to its rapid economic development during the 1960s, Japan was one of the nations to suffer severe pollution, a warning signal that the natural environment is not a bottomless dumping ground. Japan has a most vivid fear of nuclear war, having experienced nuclear destruction firsthand. In short, the Japanese are already initiated into the prerequisites of a consciousness of "our earth." In addition, as a result of the lowered cost of travel brought about by the technological revolution, the rapid development of global information networks, and the easing of restrictions on international exchanges, there is no doubt that the world is "shrinking."

As corporate activities develop more and more along international lines, the earth will become increasingly smaller to the Japanese. It is likely that Japanese employed in their companies' foreign branches will no longer view their stays only as temporary sojourns. Instead, they will attempt to deepen their contacts with the indigenous community.

As Japanese head out to all corners of the earth, they will begin to understand other societies as they really are, whether they be well-developed, under development, or extremely poor societies not yet started out on the road to development. In seeing at first hand the problems of others—problems which, in most cases, cannot be solved by the nation in question alone—Japanese will for the first time truly comprehend the problems and the vantage points of other peoples. From this process will be born a type of Japanese who has a personal feel for the global community.

At the same time, obstacles to a full realization of a sense of global community are many. The greatest are, first, the possibility of increased insularity, and, second, the problem of language.

As Japan grows more prosperous, it will come to offer the same comforts of life as the West. And as information about foreign countries becomes more readily available, people may come to be satisfied with short trips abroad or even with learning about other societies at home. Worse still, Japanese attention may turn inward, to the point where interest in things foreign decreases.

As we have stressed, however, future Japanese affluence can only be achieved by participation in the international community. It is for its own benefit that Japan must make efforts at international exchange and to develop a global perspective. Therefore, it is vital that large numbers of Japanese at some point in their lives spend considerable time abroad—through overseas work assignments, study programs and youth exchanges.

The cultivation of an international consciousness should start with children, and in this the role of schools will be significant. It would be difficult, in the context of this round-table discussion report, to set forth systematic prescriptions concerning the future role of the schools. What follows are a few suggestions for specific reforms.

First of all, there is clearly a need for the expansion of a system by which schoolteachers can gain experience in foreign countries. The teachers who will instruct students in the principles of the global community must themselves have a vivid sense of what they teach. Experiencing life abroad merely through brief group tours is not enough. A large-scale system should be instituted whereby many teachers can go abroad on their own for extended periods of time.

Next, some provision must be made by Japanese schools to fully utilize the experiences of those Japanese children who return home after long stays abroad. Having had a variety of new and unique experiences, they are particularly valuable assets to their respective schools. For the development of a global perspective among children, the experiences of these returnees should be shared with their classmates. Rather than relegating them to special schools or classes, the educational system must, at all stages and in all schools, accept and accommodate such children.

In view of the fact that language is the basis of communication, there is a need for improvement of English language instruction and for diversification in foreign language education.

We can hardly deny that, given the extent to which its use has spread across the globe, English is at present the common international language. Japanese, as members of the global community, must master English, the principal medium of global communication. English instruction in Japan's schools, however, emphasize reading and grammar, not conversation. Rote language examinations conducted at various levels serve to replicate this deficiency all the way from junior high school to university. Native English instructors should be actively recruited, and language instruction should begin at as early an age as possible. For instance, some argue that conversation-oriented English programs should begin at the primary school level, and this is worth consideration. Care should be taken, however, that young children find their English training enjoyable instead of being another burdensome round of tests. At the same time, in view of the fact that English will not be adequate for conducting all exchanges between Japan and the world, it is necessary to implement changes in the educational system that would facilitate the study of other foreign languages. The teaching of Asian languages such as Korean and Chinese is particularly important since these countries are geographically and economically close to Japan.

If the age at which English instruction begins can be lowered and the burden of examination-oriented instruction methods can be lightened, students will find moving on to other foreign languages easier. Improving the instruction of English and other foreign languages will enable the Japanese to interact more effectively with the outside world.

Conclusion

The following is a brief summary of the arguments and recommendations in the three parts of the Final Report.

Part I

A new industrial revolution is under way, and with it a new form of industrial society is in the process of being born. Not only will this significantly alter the structure of the world economy, but it will influence the political and social makeup of international society as well.

The system of global management, too, seems likely to change with the changing international environment. As we enter the 21st century, the military dominance of the United States and the Soviet Union will not change appreciably. A bipolar balance (with neither side gaining the upper hand) will be maintained. In economic terms, the nations that have dominated the world stage since the end of World War II will find it increasingly difficult to bear the burden of international economic stability. The rapid deepening of international interdependence occasioned by the development of trade and industry under the liberal postwar economic system has increased mutual understanding, but at the same time has raised the number of parties involved in international exchange and exacerbated economic and other frictions.

In the years ahead, each nation must bear a share of the costs of international public goods and work together in constructing a new global management system. Under this system, each nation would not give priority to its own profits alone, but would act as a flexible coordinator of interests within and without its borders and cooperate in building a better international order. The people of each nation must raise their consciousness of the need for cooperation and solidarity transcending national boundaries. A consciousness of global community will be needed.

Sheltered by the free economic system of the postwar era, Japan has grown to wield great influence in the world economy. To contribute to future world prosperity and peace, Japan must consider its role in and contributions to the global community. Internationalization that builds on the characteristics of Japanese culture is being demanded of Japan in order that its ties to international society may be strengthened.

Part II

Japanese policy must proceed in three basic directions, given the nation's place in the global community on the eve of the 21st century.

First, Japan must cease to act as a minor power and passive bystander in world affairs. It must become of its own accord one of the principal supporters of the system of collective management and assume its share of the burden of providing international public goods. To this end, Japan should itself take up the idea of the global community and strive to balance its profit with that of other nations.

Second, Japan should pursue its development in harmony with the world in such a way that, while achieving sufficient economic growth, it can use its economic vitality to contribute to the development of the global community, not only in the economic sense but in other senses, including culture, as well. It can become an economic and cultural contributor to the global community.

Third, as an Asian country, Japan can contribute greatly to regional stability and economic growth in Asia. It should promote an open system of regional cooperation (cooperation in energy and information programs, etc.) and balanced economic, cultural, and human interdependence that gives full rein to the economic vitality of Asia, which, in turn, will contribute to overall world growth.

The following seven points constitute a proposal for specific ways in which Japan can fulfill its role in and contribute to the global community.

1. Further Expansion of Free Trade

The benefits of free trade must be equally available to all. Further liberalization of imports of products now exempted under the GATT system is needed to secure export opportunities for developing countries. Japan should take active steps to open its own markets.

To facilitate emergency industrial adjustment for declining and other industries and development policies for high-tech industries, a new international order should be sought. The purpose of this order would be to maintain international competition and to forestall any disruptions of trade.

2. Toward Structural Policy Coordination

In order to stabilize the international monetary situation and to adjust macro-economic imbalances, international policy coordination in the fiscal and monetary areas should be actively encouraged. We must lay the groundwork for such policy coordination.

3. Encouraging Mutually Beneficial Direct Investment

To make full use of Japan's savings surplus and managerial resources, direct investment should be encouraged. Direct investment is desirable because it is a superior method of transferring skills and technology through human interaction.

In order to ensure that direct investment is well received by the host country and subsequently contributes to its development, an appropriate distribution of profits between investor and host must be encouraged. Likewise, training of local technicians and employment and promotion of local people will be vital.

4. Japanese Corporations and Internationalization

The institutional methods that have characterized Japanese corporations in the past, including lifetime employment, may well change significantly in the process of internationalization and in the face of the trends of the new age. Some international convergence of management methods is likely to take place.

It is important for Japanese corporations to, while making organizational adjustments, hold to the basic tenet that has guided their development thus far—the principle that people are the most fundamental source of a firm's economic activity.

5. Human, Scientific, and Technological Exchanges

In order to promote balanced mutual exchange and to increase opportunities for day-to-day interaction, as well as to deepen mutual understanding, Japan must make itself a locus for human, scientific and technological, and educational exchange.

This will entail a fundamental expansion of the system for accepting foreign students and trainees through such measures as the establishment of a study/human exchange program and flexible adjustment of school terms. The system for training engineers from developing countries needs to be strengthened, access to national research facilities improved, a "working holiday" system expanded, and facilities for Japanese language training, both in Japan and overseas, upgraded.

6. Responding to North-South Problems

To assist in the independent development of the South, economic and technological cooperation with developing countries —at both public and private levels—must be given renewed emphasis. The opening of markets in developed countries and prevention of wide and rapid fluctuation in exchange rates should be given priority.

While recognizing the importance of coming to grips with the population problem, Japan should send necessary relief to victims of dire poverty and famine. In addition, Japan should support afforestation and other land-use programs.

7. Security and World Peace

Japan should consolidate its defense systems, while retaining a defense-oriented posture. Equally important will be the creation of regional—and, by extension, international—political stability through cooperative economic relations. Japan should also reaffirm its support for international organizations as a means of encouraging peace and resolving international disputes.

Part III

For Japan to be more closely tied to the international community in the coming decades, it will be vital that, first, Japanese enjoy a more balanced affluence and have the leeway to take on part of the burden of contributing to global progress. Second,

Japanese must learn to accept diverse value systems and to co-exist with people who have different lifestyles. Third, the people of Japan must open their hearts to the world to develop a true feeling of global community. Instead of waiting passively for outside influence to trickle in, or for generational transitions to bring reformed thinking, the Japanese must improve housing, social capital and other elements of infrastructure and implement changes in social systems, customs, education (especially English language education), and other areas.

Final Remarks

This report is built around the matters that proved of most interest to Round Table members, but it does not necessarily give systematic consideration to all of the problems raised. The role and contribution of "Japan in the Global Community" as described in this report should not, therefore, be taken as being comprehensive.

The purpose of this report is not limited to outlining Japan's role in and contributions to the future world. As argued above, it is extremely important that Japan clearly recognize its present position in the world; on the basis of this recognition, it can make adjustments in domestic interests and develop a long-term international perspective, through which Japan's interest will be harmonized with those of the world. To this end, this report is published to stimulate wide-ranging discussions among governments, corporations, and individuals, in the hope that such discussion will lead to more concrete responses to the problems mentioned herein. We believe that in this world of increasing interdependence, Japan can pursue a course of long-term development together with nations of the world, and that in time a true global community can become an actuality.

ROUND TABLE DISCUSSION ON JAPAN IN THE GLOBAL COMMUNITY

Schedule of Discussions

1st Round Table Discussion September 4, 1985 (Wednesday)	Perspectives on Japan in the Global Community as We Approach the 21st Century; Short Proposals by Members
2nd Round Table Discussion October 22, 1985 (Tuesday)	Transformation of the International System and the Position of Japan * How is the present international system changing, and how will it continue to change into the 21st century? * What will be Japan's position in the global community, and in what spheres (international political economy, security, culture, etc.) should Japan contribute to the global community? (including the position and role of Japan in North-South and East-West relations, Japan in Asia and the Pacific Basin)
3rd Round Table Discussion November 19, 1985 (Tuesday)	Role and Contribution Required of Japan in the Global Community with Regard to Trade, Monetary and Financial Systems, and Economic Policy * Stabilization of international trade and the international financial and monetary systems * Harmonizing economic policy management internationally
4th Round Table Discussion December 17, 1985 (Tuesday)	1. Role and Contribution Required of Japan in the Global Community with Regard to the Maintenance of Peace, Security, and the Solution of the North-South Problem (Economic Cooperation)

	2. Role and Contribution Required of Japan in the Global Community with Regard to International Mutual Understanding and the Promotion of Exchange
	  * International human exchange by engineers, researchers, business people, teachers and students
	  * International cultural exchange
	  * Mutual understanding of social customs, systems, and philosophies

5th Round Table Discussion
January 20, 1986 (Monday)
	Role and Contribution of Japanese Firms in the Global Community
	  * Trade, investment and technology
	  * Enterprise management, local activities and international conduct that accord with world conditions
	  * Exchange with local societies and cultures by means of enterprise activities

6th Round Table Discussion
February 18, 1986 (Tuesday)
	Image of the Japanese People in the Global Community and the Japanese Social System
	  * The place of the Japanese economic community in the history of civilization and the transformation of industrial society
	  * Awareness and understanding within Japanese society of "Japan in the Global Community"

Working Group February 17, 1986 (Monday)	I. Transformation of the International System and the Position of Japan II. Trade, Monetary and Financial Systems, International Economic Relations, and Business Enterprises
February 19, 1986 (Wednesday)	III. International Human Exchange, Social Systems and Culture

| 7th Round Table Discussion
April 7, 1986 (Monday) | Discussion of the Draft Report |
| 8th Round Table Discussion
April 18, 1986 (Friday) | Presentation of the Draft Report |

Supplementary Figures and Tables

1. World GNP Shares (1982)

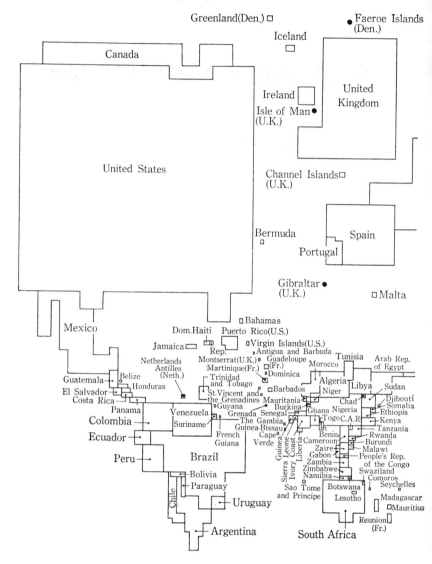

Source: International Bank for Reconstruction and Development, *Atlas.*

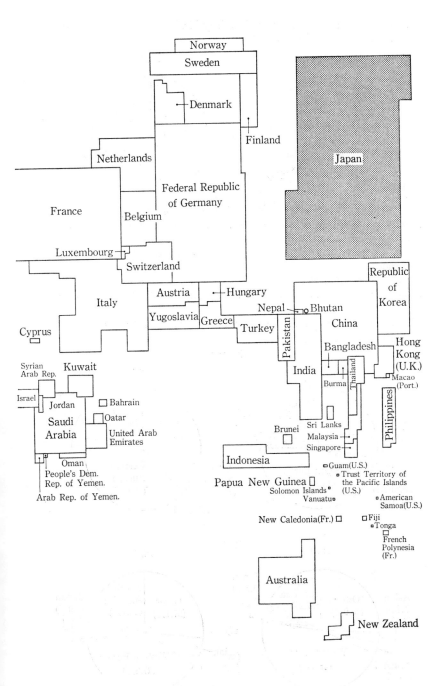

2. Change in GNP Share of Leading Nations and Major Regions of the World, 1970 to 1982

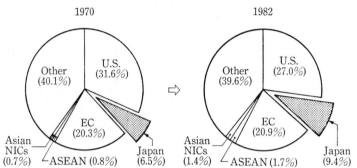

Notes: 1. Each share represents percentages of world GNP (based on nominal GNP converted into U.S. dollars).

2. ASEAN: Indonesia, Malaysia, Philippines, and Thailand (Brunei is excluded).

3. Asian NICs: Hong Kong, Republic of Korea, Singapore, and Taiwan.

Sources: United Nations, *Yearbook of National Accounts*; Asian Development Bank.

3. Shift in Foreign Trade Shares of Leading Nations and Major Regions, 1970 to 1984

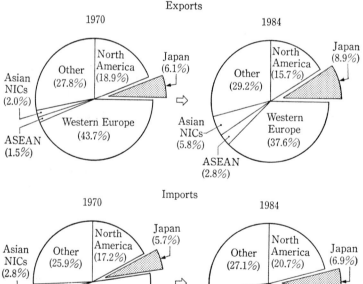

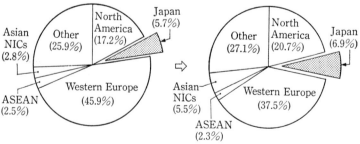

4. Direct Foreign Investment, 1984

A. Balance of Direct Foreign Investment (stock base)

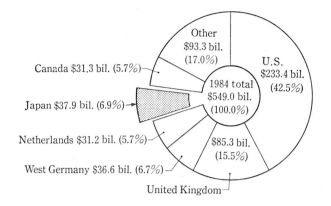

Notes: 1. Balance of investment converted into U.S. dollars at year-end rate.
2. World total estimates by Japan External Trade Organization.
Source: JETRO, *The World and Japanese Direct Foreign Investment* (1986).

B. Balance of Direct Foreign Investment (flow base)

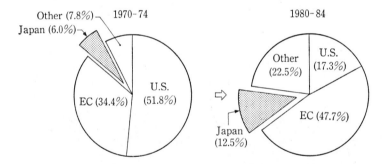

Sources: OECD, *Recent International Direct Investment Trends;* Bank of England, *Quarterly Bulletin*; De Nederlandsche Bank, n.v., *Quarterly Statistics, Survey of Current Business*; IMF, *IFS, Balance of Payments Statistics, Balance of Payments Monthly*; Ministry of Finance, JETRO, *The World and Japanese Direct Foreign Investment* (1986); MITI, *White Paper on International Trade* (1986).

Notes: 1. ASEAN: Indonesia, Malaysia, Philippines, and Thailand (Brunei is excluded).
2. Asian NICs: Hong Kong, Republic of Korea, Singapore, and Taiwan.
Source: Economic Planning Agency, *White Paper on the Global Economy* (1985), based on the United Nations, *Monthly Bulletin of Statistics*.

5. Foreign Currency Composition of Japan's National Reserves, 1984

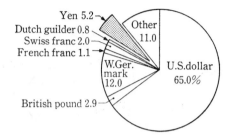

Note: Foreign currency reserves of the Japanese government and central banks. These figures plus gold, IMF reserve position, and special drawing rights constitute the country's foreign currency reserves.
Source: International Monetary Fund, *Annual Report, 1985.*

6. Major DAC Nations' Expenditures for Economic Cooperation and Official Development Assistance, 1984

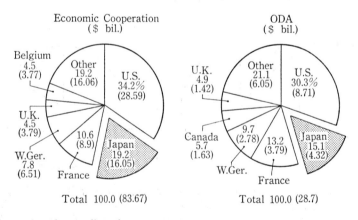

Note: Actual expenditure base.
Source: Development Assistance Committee, OECD.

7. Share of Support for United Nations, 1970 and 1985

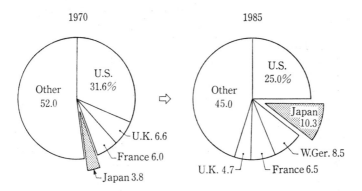

Note: Operating expenses of the United Nations are covered by member nations. The proportion of funds to be provided by each nation is determined in a meeting of the General Assembly every two years.

Source: *The Statesman's Yearbook.*

8. Trends in Real Economic Growth of Leading Nations

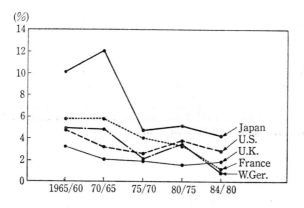

Source: Bank of Japan, *International Comparison Statistics.*

9. Export Trends for Leading Nations

	Average annual growth rate (%)		
	1950–60	1960–70	1970–81
Advanced countries			
U.S.	5.3	6.2	6.4
Canada	3.8	9.5	4.1
Australia	5.0	6.7	3.6
New Zealand	2.6	5.2	4.3
Japan	10.6	15.8	10.7
Asian NICs			
Korea	7.1	19.3	10.5
Taiwan	—	20.1	17.0
Hong Kong	—	12.5	10.3
Singapore	—	7.1	11.9
ASEAN			
Indonesia	4.9	3.6	6.8
Malaysia	—	5.8	8.2
Philippines	3.9	5.8	7.2
Thailand	5.4	10.5	9.4
China	—	—	20.2
Latin America			
Mexico	4.5	5.4	8.2
Peru	9.6	3.2	−0.3
Ecuador	—	−0.1	10.4
Columbia	4.9	3.8	5.3
Europe			
U.K.	3.0	4.8	4.0
France	7.0	8.4	7.6
West Germany	15.1	8.2	6.0

Source: World Bank, *World Tables*, 3rd ed., *1984*. *Taiwan Statistical Data Book*, *1984*. IMF, *International Financial Statistics*.

10. Trends in Balance of Trade for Leading Nations and Major Regions

(unit: $ bil.)

Region / Year	1981	1982	1983	1984	1985
OECD	−27.8	−21.2	−16.4	−42.2	−53.0
Group of Seven indus- trialized nations	1.7	3.8	− 5.0	−39.8	−49.0
U.S.	−27.9	−36.5	− 6.2	−108.3	−129.0
Canada	6.6	15.0	14.9	16.6	−14.0
Japan	20.0	18.1	31.5	43.3	54.0
EC	− 4.1	3.1	10.6	9.4	14.0
France	−10.1	−15.5	− 8.2	− 4.1	− 4.5
West Germany	17.9	26.7	23.3	23.3	29.3
Italy	−10.6	− 8.0	3.1	− 6.1	−10.3
U.K.	6.0	4.1	− 1.3	− 5.5	− 2.8
Non-oil producing developing nations	−70.0	−45.0	−20.0	1.0	− 1.0
Oil-producing nations	− 4.0	2.0	9.0	12.0	10.0
Communist bloc nations	13.0	22.0	23.0	24.0	3.0

Notes: 1. Figures for 1985 are based on GATT estimates for the Communist bloc and on OECD estimates for all other regions.

2. Communist bloc figures are FOB-CIF base; remainder are IMF base.

Source: MITI *White Paper on International Trade* (1986) drawing on OECD, *Economic Outlook* and GATT, *International Trade*.

11. Unemployment Rate Trends

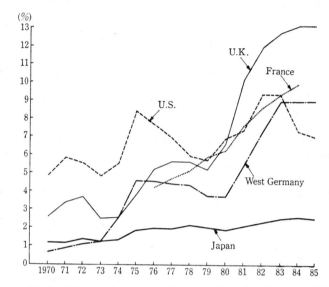

Sources: Bank of Japan, *International Comparison Statistics;* Economic Planning
Agency, *Indices of External Economic Trends.*

12. Labor Productivity Growth Rate

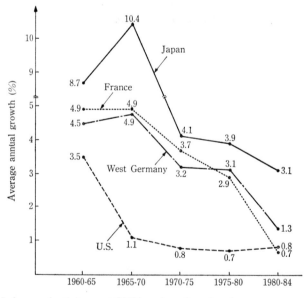

Note: Labor productivity=net GNP/number of employed persons.
Source: Bank of Japan, *International Comparison Statistics* (1985).

13. Changing Rates of Customs Duties

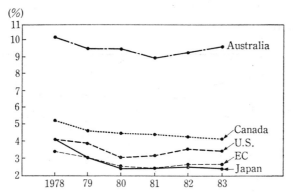

Note: Rate=amount of customs revenue/value of imports.
Source: MITI, *White Paper on International Trade* (1986).

14. Effects of the Kennedy and Tokyo Rounds

Kennedy Round (1964–67)	Customs duty rate on taxable items in 1966	20.5%
	Customs duty rate on taxable items in 1973	10.2%

		Rate of nominal customs duty for tariffed commodities				Rate of nominal customs duty for all commodities including those non-tariffed		
		Japan	U.S.	EC		Japan	U.S.	EC
Tokyo Round (1973–79)	Standard customs duty rate	9.9%	8.2%	9.7%	Standard customs duty rate	5.8%	6.0%	6.4%
	Actual customs duty rate	6.9	8.2	9.7	Actual customs duty rate	3.7	6.0	6.4
	After rate reduction	5.5	6.0	7.0	After rate reduction	3.0	4.0	5.0

Notes: 1. Total of mineral and industrial products excluding petroleum.
 2. Weighted average value of imports from the world in 1976 is used.
 3. Standard customs duty rate=rate used as basis for negotiating rate reductions.
 4. Actual customs duty rate=most-favored-nation rate for GATT members as of April 1, 1979.
Source: Ministry of International Trade and Industry.

15. Trends in Leading Nations' Share of High Technology Product Trade in OECD Total

Exports

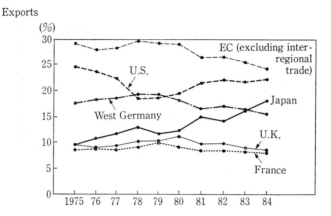

Imports

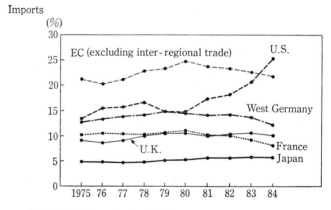

Source: OECD, *Statistics on Foreign Trade.*

16. Trends in Ratio of R&D Expenditures to GNP

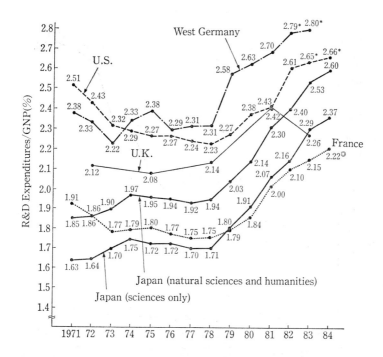

Notes: Data are R&D totals for natural sciences, social sciences and humanities.
Asterisks indicate estimated figures. Double circles indicate rough estimates.

Sources: Compiled by Ministry of International Trade and Industry based on the following materials:

Japan: General Affairs Agency, 1981–83 Survey Reports and "Outline of Scientific and Technological Research, 1984," and Economic Planning Agency, "1980 Standard Revised National Economic Accounting," "1983 National Economic Accounting."

U.S.: N.S.F., *National Patterns of Science and Technology Resources.*

West Germany: *Bundesministerium Fur Forschung und Technologie Bundesbericht Forschung, 1984.*

U.K.: *Cabinet Office, Annual Review of Government Funded R&D.*

France: Ministère de l'Economie, des Finances et du Budget, *Projet de Loi de Finances Pour 1986.*

17. Trends in Foreign Trade Balance and Technology Trade Ratio

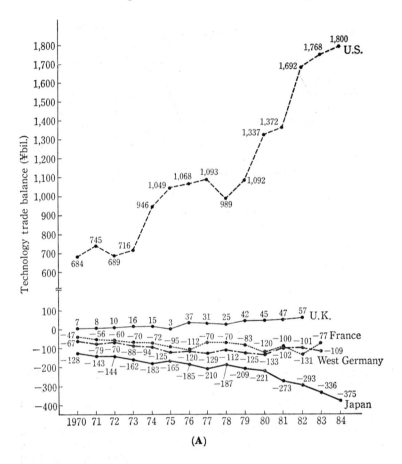

(A)

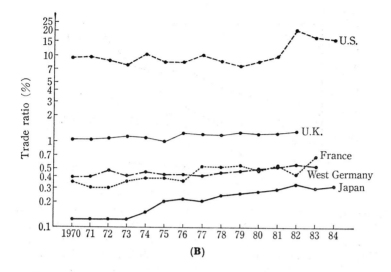

(B)

Notes: 1. Technology trade consists of transactions in the form of assignments, licensing, etc., of the fruits of R&D activity in scientific technologies.

2. U.S. figures for 1982, 1983, 1984 technology exports include rental fees for movie films.

3. Trade ratio=export value/import value.

Sources: Science and Technology Agency, *White Paper on Science and Technology* (1985) based on the following documents:

Japan: Bank of Japan, *Balance of Payments Monthly.*

U.S.: Department of Commerce, *Survey of Current Business* (N.S.B.); *Science Indicators—1982.*

U.K.: Department of Industry, *Business Monitor, MA4—Overseas Transactions.*

West Germany: Bundes Bank, *Monatsbericht der Deutsche Bundesbank.*

France: Ministère de l'Economie, des Finances et du Budget, *Statistiques & Etudes Financieres.*

18. World Military Expenditures

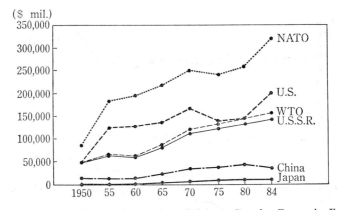

Notes: 1. 12 NATO member nations: Belgium, Canada, Denmark, France, Ireland, Italy, Luxemburg, Netherlands, Norway, Portugal, U.K., U.S.A.
 2. 7 Warsaw Treaty Organization (WTO) member nations: Bulgaria, Hungary, G.D.R. Germany, Poland, Romania, U.S.S.R., Czechoslovakia.
 3, Figures are in million US$ at 1981 price and exchange rates.
Source: International Peace Research Institute, Stockholm.

19. Ratio of Military Expenditures to GNP in Leading Nations

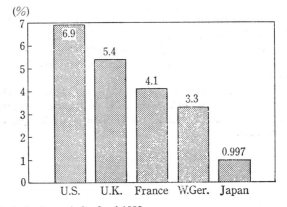

Note: Ratio for Japan is for fiscal 1985.
Source: Defense Agency, *Defense of Japan* (1985).

20. Percentage of Energy Self-sufficiency of Leading Nations (1984)

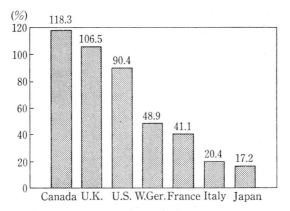

Source: OECD, *Energy Balance.*

21. Ratio of Grain Self-sufficiency for Leading Nations (1982)

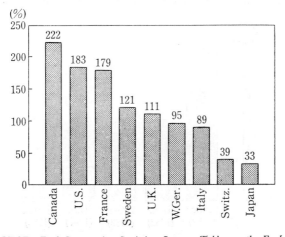

Source: OECD, *Food Consumption Statistics*; Japan, *Tables on the Food Supply.*

22. Number of Foreign Students Enrolled in Institutions of Higher Education

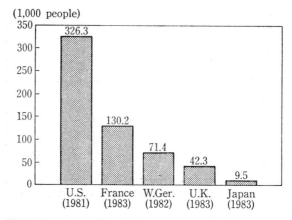

(1,000 people)

Source: UNESCO, *Statistical Yearbook.*

23. Ratio of Foreign Students in Institutions of Higher Education

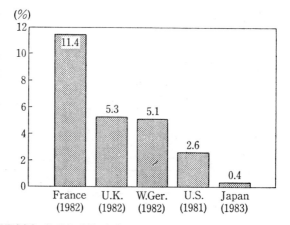

(%)

Source: UNESCO, *Statistical Yearbook.*

24. International Comparison of Annual Man-hours Worked

1. Total Real Man-hours Worked (1984)

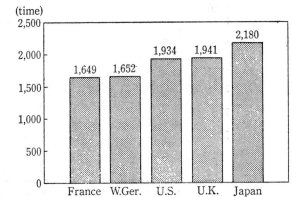

2. Holidays (1983)

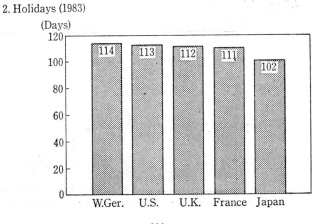

(A)

Paid Vacation Taken (1983)

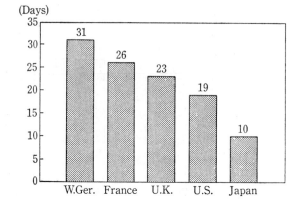

4. Days of Absence

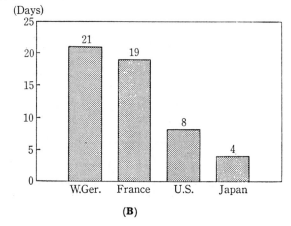

(B)

Note: Number of days absent excluding paid annual vacation and regular holi-
days.

Source: Compiled by Japanese Ministry of Labor using documents from each
individual country.

25. International Comparison of Private Housing and Accumulation of Social Capital

1. Ratio of Total Population with Access to Sewage Facilities

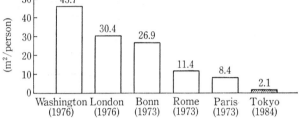

2. Municipal Park Space Per Capita

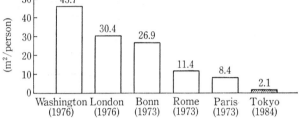

3. Additions to Express Highways per 10,000 Automobiles in One Year

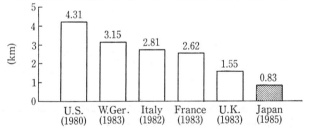

4. Average Number of Occupants per Room

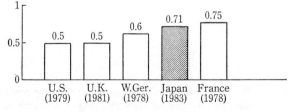

Source: Ministry of Construction, *White Paper on Construction.*

26. Dependence on Foreign Trade of Leading Nations and Major Regions

Exports.

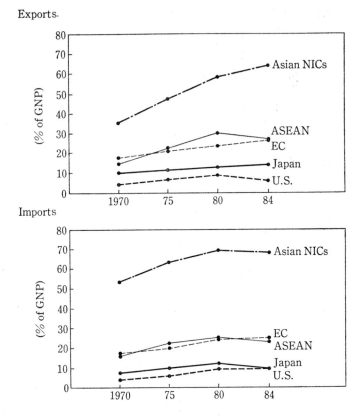

Imports

Note: Brunei is excluded from ASEAN and Taiwan from the Asian NICs as a result of constraints on availability of data.

Source: IMF, *International Financial Statistics.*

Notes: (a) Long-term capital only (term exceeding one-year period). (b) Including increase and decrease of short- and long-term reserves in foreign currency.

Source: Economic Planning Agency, *White Paper on the Global Economy* (1984), based on U.S. Department of Commerce, *Survey of Current Business*; Bank of England, *Quarterly Bulletin*; and Bank of Japan, *Balance of Payments Monthly.*

27. Trade Relationships among Major Regions   **28.** Capital Movements among Major Regions

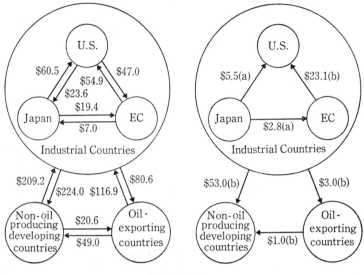

(Unit: $ bil.)

(27)
Note: Figures are FOB export prices in billion U.S. dollars (1984).
Source: IMF, *Direction of Trade Statistics*, 1985. OECD, *Monthly Statistics of Foreign Trade*, March 1986.

29. International Subscriber-Dialed Telephone Calls from Japan

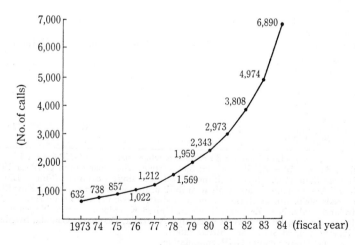

Source: Ministry of Posts and Telecommunications, *White Paper on Communications* (1985).

30. Numbers of Overseas Travelers Entering Japan and of Japanese Traveling Abroad

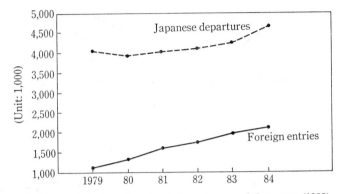

Source: Ministry of Justice, *Annual Report on Entries and Departures* (1985).

31. Basic Data on Developing Countries

	Developing countries				Market economy industrial countries (d)
	Low income (a)	Middle income (b)	High income oil-exporting (c)	Total (a) + (b) + (c)	
Population (million) (1983)	2,335.4	1,165.2	17.9	3,518.5	728.9
Area (million km²)	31.6	40.5	4.3	76.4	30.9
GNP (1983) ($100 million)	607.2	1,526.4	221.4	2,355.0	8,061.6
GNP per capita ($; 1983)	260	1,310	12,370	669	11,060
Exports (1983) (F.O.B.; $1 billion)	46.0	333.5	120.8	500.3	1,128.1
Average life span at time of birth (years; 1983)	59	61	59	60	76
Proportion of population in cities (%; 1983)	22	43	68	31	77

Notes: 1. (a)=Low income: 35 countries where per capita GNP for 1983 is less than $400. (b)=Middle income: 59 countries where per capita GNP for 1983 is more than $400. (c)=High income oil-exporting: 5 countries (Oman, Libya, Saudi Arabia, Kuwait, and United Arab Emirates) where per capita GNP for 1983 exceeds $600. (d)=Market economy industrial countries: 19 countries (Spain, Ireland, Italy, New Zealand, Belgium, United Kingdom, Austria, Netherlands, Japan, France, Finland, West Germany, Australia, Denmark, Canada, Sweden, Norway, United States, and Switzerland).
2. GNP=per capita GNP×population.
Source: World Bank, *World Development Report* (1985).

32. Increase Rates in Per Capita GNP (1975)

	1960–70	1970–80	1977	1978	1979	1980	1981
Developing countries as a whole	2.9	3.3	3.1	2.2	2.1	0.2	−2.2
Major oil exporting countries (a)	3.8	3.7	2.9	2.2	3.0	−3.1	−4.9
Rapidly growing manufactured product exporting countries (b)	3.0	4.7	3.6	1.9	5.2	3.1	−4.0
Least less-developed countries (LLDC)	0.9	1.2	1.4	−2.1	0.3	−0.3	1.0
Other	2.2	2.0	3.1	2.8	−0.9	1.9	1.5
Industrialized countries (c)	3.7	2.5	3.3	3.5	2.8	0.0	0.7
Socialist countries (Eastern Europe) (d)	5.6	4.4	3.9	3.8	1.2	1.7	0.9

Notes: (a)=21 countries (Algeria, Angola, Bahrain, Brunei, Congo, Ecuador, Gabon, Indonesia, Iran, Iraq, Kuwait, Libya, Mexico, Nigeria, Oman, Qater, Saudi Arabia, Syria, Trinidad-Tobago, United Arab Emirates, and Venezuela).

(b)=6 countries (Argentina, Brazil, (Hong Kong), South Korea, Singapore and (Taiwan).

(c)=Development Assistance Committee (DAC) member countries as well as Greece, Luxembourg, Ireland, Iceland, (Faeroe Islands), Portugal, Spain, Yugoslavia, Israel, and South Africa.

(d)=Albania, Bulgaria, Czechoslovakia, G.D.R. Germany, Hungary, Poland, Romania, and U.S.S.R.

Source: Ministry of Foreign Affairs, *Recent Issues in Japan's Foreign Affairs* (1985).

33. Trends in the Real GDP Growth Rate of Non-Oil-Exporting Developing Countries

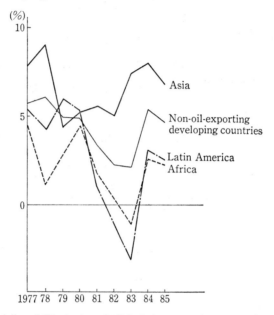

Note: "Asia" and "Latin America" include some oil-exporting countries.
Source: IMF, *World Economic Outlook, October 1985.*

34. Trends in Debt Balance of Developing Countries

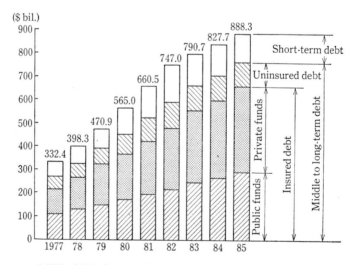

Source: MITI, *White Paper on International Trade* (1986), based on IMF, *World Economic Outlook.*

35. Export Structure of the Non-Oil-Producing Developing
Countries and the Industrialized Countries

Non-oil-producing developing countries

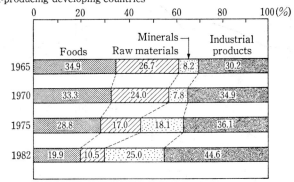

Industrialized countries

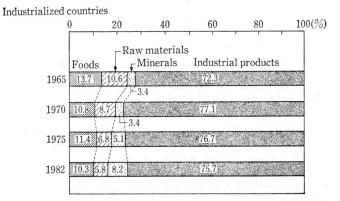

Notes: 1. Number indicates share in each category.
2. SITC classification.
Source: United Nations, *Yearbook of International Trade Statistics.*

36. World Trends in Grain
Production, 1979–84

37. Grain Production in
African Developing Areas

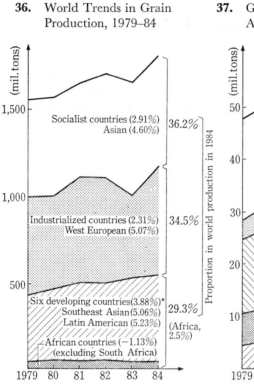

*South Korea, India, Thailand, Indonesia, Malaysia, and Philippines.

Note: The average increase rate for
1979–84 is 2.97%. Figures in parentheses are average increase rates for
each region.

Source: MITI, *White Paper on Economic Cooperation* (1985), based on
FAO, *Production Yearbook 1984*.

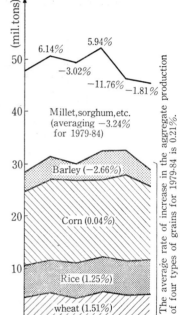

Note: The average increase rate for
1979–84 is −1.13%.

Source: *See* 36.

38. Major Japanese Economic Indicators

Year	National Income (by distributive share)			Trade Income (customs basis)	
	Total (¥ bil.)	Increase rate over previous year (%)	Per capita (¥1,000)	Exports ($ mil.)	Imports ($ mil.)
1955	7,298.5	—	82	2,137	2,586
1960	13,269.1	20.4	142	4,116	4,660
1961	15,755.1	18.7	167	4,321	6,009
1962	17,729.8	12.5	186	5,009	5,622
1963	20,627.1	16.3	215	5,636	7,247
1964	23,390.4	13.4	241	7,187	7,921
1965	26,604.5	—	269	8,724	8,417
1966	31,104.9	16.9	314	9,958	10,019
1967	36,776.5	18.2	369	10,774	12,061
1968	43,124.9	17.3	423	13,671	13,290
1969	50,859.1	17.9	502	16,798	16,003
1970	61,029.7	18.7	589	20,250	19,353
1971	65,910.5	8.0	627	25,124	20,251
1972	77,936.9	18.2	726	29,994	25,362
1973	95,839.6	23.0	879	39,679	44,948
1974	112,471.6	17.4	1,018	58,390	62,613
1975	123,990.7	10.2	1,109	56,982	58,225
1976	140,397.2	13.2	1,242	70,577	67,284
1977	155,703.2	10.9	1,365	84,625	71,668
1978	171,778.5	10.3	1,492	98,969	84,635
1979	182,206.9	6.1	1,570	107,020	120,471
1980	199,335.2	9.4	1,704	138,058	143,976
1981	208,156.6	4.4	1,767	151,938	142,734
1982	216,859.1	4.2	1,828	136,640	127,313
1983	227,916.2	5.1	1,909	152,679	129,351
1984	239,757.1	5.2	1,995	169,619	134,528

Sources: Economic Planning Agency, *Report on Revised National Accounts;* Ministry of Finance, *Foreign Trade Statistics.*

39. Changes in Economic Indicators, 1951–84

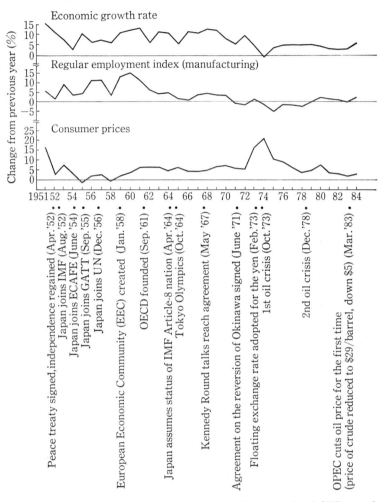

Notes: 1. "Economic growth rate" is the rate of increase of real GNP over the previous year.

2. The rates for 1951–65 were obtained through the old System of National Accounts; those for 1966 and after, through the new SNA. 1980 values are used for 1970 and after.

Source: Economic Planning Agency, *Outline of the Economy* (1985).

40. Component Ratio of Japanese Imports and Exports by Region, 1985

Exports ($ mil., f.o.b.)

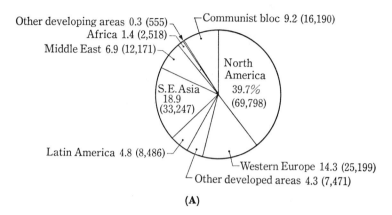

Other developing areas 0.3 (555)
Africa 1.4 (2,518)
Middle East 6.9 (12,171)
Communist bloc 9.2 (16,190)
North America 39.7% (69,798)
S.E.Asia 18.9 (33,247)
Latin America 4.8 (8,486)
Western Europe 14.3 (25,199)
Other developed areas 4.3 (7,471)

(A)

Imports ($ mil., c.i.f.)

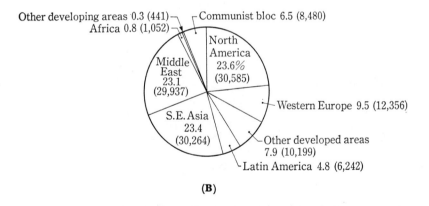

Other developing areas 0.3 (441)
Africa 0.8 (1,052)
Communist bloc 6.5 (8,480)
North America 23.6% (30,585)
Middle East 23.1 (29,937)
Western Europe 9.5 (12,356)
S.E.Asia 23.4 (30,264)
Other developed areas 7.9 (10,199)
Latin America 4.8 (6,242)

(B)

Source: Japan Tariff Association, *Summary Report, Trade of Japan.*

41. Component Ratio of Japan's Imports and Exports by Product, 1985

Exports ($ mil., f.o.b.)

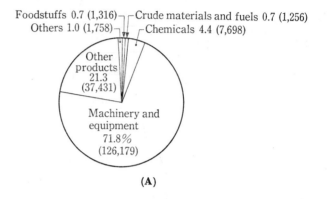

Foodstuffs 0.7 (1,316) — ┌ Crude materials and fuels 0.7 (1,256)
Others 1.0 (1,758) — ↓↓ ┌ Chemicals 4.4 (7,698)

Other products 21.3 (37,431)

Machinery and equipment 71.8% (126,179)

(A)

Imports ($ mil., c.i.f.)

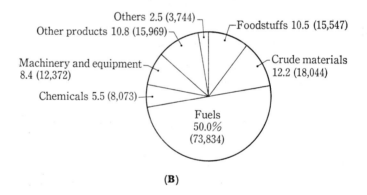

Others 2.5 (3,744) ─┐ ┌ Foodstuffs 10.5 (15,547)
Other products 10.8 (15,969) ─┐
Machinery and equipment 8.4 (12,372) ─
Crude materials 12.2 (18,044)
Chemicals 5.5 (8,073) ─

Fuels 50.0% (73,834)

(B)

Source: Japan Tariff Association, *Summary Report, Trade of Japan.*

42. Trends in Japan's Trade Balance by Region

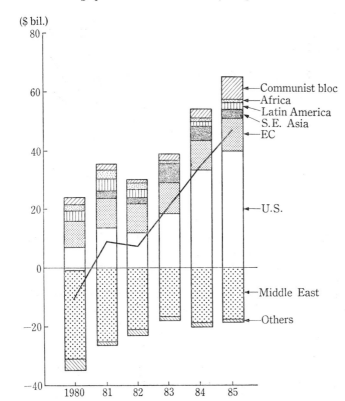

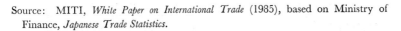

Source: MITI, *White Paper on International Trade* (1985), based on Ministry of Finance, *Japanese Trade Statistics.*

43. Japanese Domestic Production, Exports, and Direct Overseas Investment

(1970=100)   (dollar basis)

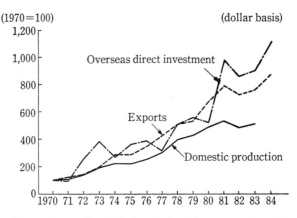

Notes: 1. "Domestic production" is obtained by converting shipment of manufactured products into dollars.

2. "Direct overseas investment" is computed on a fiscal-year base from reported figures.

Source: MITI, *White Paper on International Trade* (1986), based on Ministry of Finance, *Japanese Trade Statistics* and *Census of Manufactures*.

44. Trends in the Share of Japanese Manufacturer Direct Investment Overseas by Region

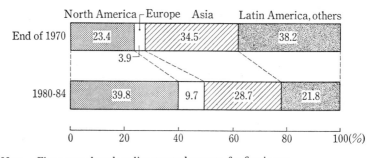

Note: Figures are based on licenses and reports, for fiscal year.

Source: MITI, *White Paper on International Trade* (1986), based on Ministry of Finance materials.

45. Trends in Japanese Direct Overseas Investment by Industry

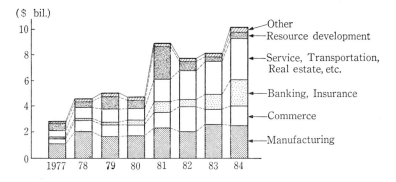

Note: License/reporting basis.
Source: MITI, *White Paper on International Trade* (1986), based on Ministry of Finance materials.

46. Employment of Foreigners by Japanese Corporations

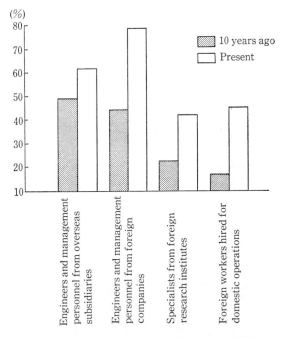

Note: Percentage is proportion of surveyed corporations which responded that they had actually hired one or more foreigners.
Source: MITI, *White Paper on International Trade* (1986), based on MITI, *Questionnaire on Internationalization of Japanese Corporations,* and Bank of Japan, *A Study of Management of Major Corporations.*

47. Trends in Japanese Direct Investment

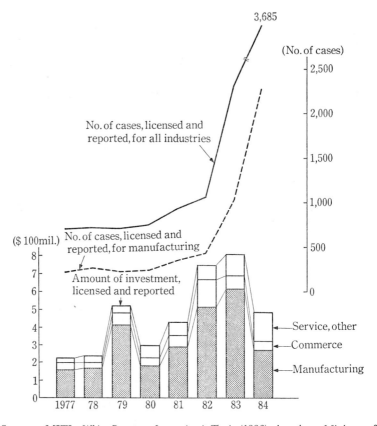

Source: MITI, *White Paper on International Trade* (1986), based on Ministry of Finance documents.

48. Trends in Japanese Economic Aid

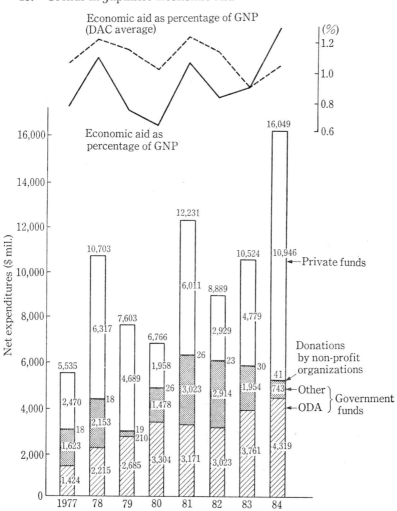

Source: MITI, *White Paper on International Trade* (1986), based on OECD, *Development Co-operation.*

49. Regional Distribution of Japan's Bilateral Economic Cooperation (Net Expenditures) ($ mil.)
(Figures in parentheses are percentages)

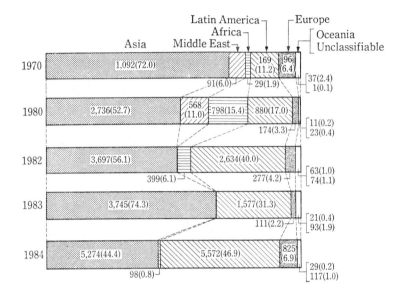

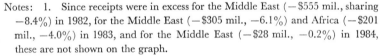

Notes: 1. Since receipts were in excess for the Middle East (−$555 mil., sharing
−8.4%) in 1982, for the Middle East (−$305 mil., −6.1%) and Africa (−$201
mil., −4.0%) in 1983, and for the Middle East (−$28 mil., −0.2%) in 1984,
these are not shown on the graph.

2. Asia in the DAC classification includes the Middle East, but in the graph
the Middle East is treated separately.

Source: MITI, *White Paper on Economic Cooperation* (1985) based on DAC data.

50. Trends in Japanese Technological Cooperation

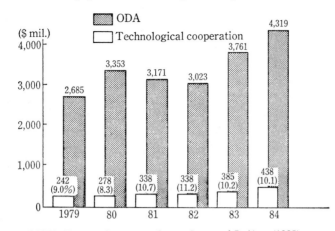

Source: MITI, *Economic Cooperation: Current Status and Problems* (1985).

51. Internationalization of the Yen

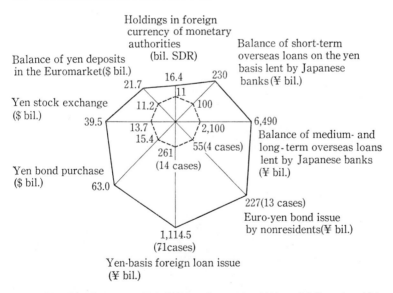

Note: The dotted lines (inside) indicate figures for 1980; solid lines (outside), for 1984.

Source: MITI, *White Paper on International Trade* (1986), based on IMF, IFS, BIS, *Quarterly Report;* Ministry of Finance, *The International Finance Bureau's Annual Report*, and *Monthly Report on the Statistics of International Balance of Payments.*